MW01620721

ANCHORED
IN
GOD
P.K.

By the Same Author

A DIALOGUE BETWEEN
BERGSON, ARISTOTLE, AND PHILOLOGOS

BYZANTINE SACRED ART

ΤΟ ΣΥΜΠΑΝ ΚΑΙ Ο ΑΝΘΡΩΠΟΣ
ΣΤΗΝ ΑΜΕΡΙΚΑΝΙΚΗ ΦΙΛΟΣΟΦΙΑ

ST. ATHANASIOS THE ATHONITE,
WHO FOUNDED THE FIRST MONASTERY ON ATHOS, IN 963
Fresco by Panselinos (XIVth cent.), Church of the Protaton, Athos

ANCHORED IN GOD

AN INSIDE ACCOUNT OF
LIFE, ART, AND THOUGHT
ON THE HOLY MOUNTAIN OF ATHOS

BY
CONSTANTINE CAVARNOS

INSTITUTE FOR BYZANTINE
AND MODERN GREEK STUDIES
115 Gilbert Road
Belmont, Massachusetts 02178

Second Printing, 2020

First published in 1959 by "ASTIR" Publishing Company, Athens, Greece
Second edition 1975, by THE INSTITUTE FOR BYZANTINE AND MODERN GREEK STUDIES, INC.
115 Gilbert Road, Belmont, Massachusetts 02178, U.S.A.
Printed in the United States of America
Library of Congress Catalog Number: 75-35432

Clothbound ISBN 0-914744-30-5
Paperbound ISBN 0-914744-31-3

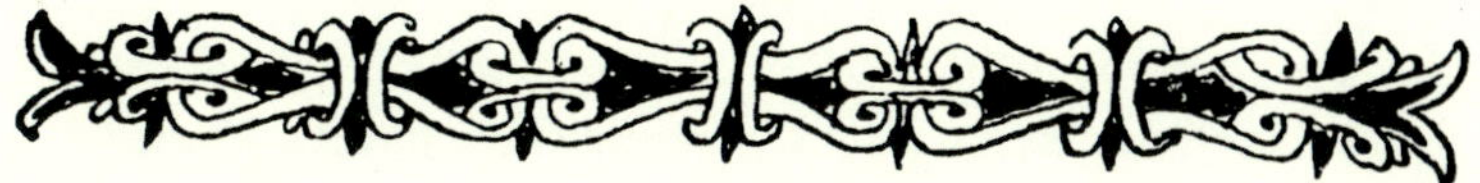

PREFACE

This book is a result of three journeys to the Holy Mountain of Athos: one in 1952, another in 1954, and a third in 1958. I have drawn mostly from the experiences and observations of my last two journeys, because I took very few notes during my first visit, whereas I kept a full account of what I saw, heard, felt, and thought during the second and third.

The purpose of these journeys was to acquire a better knowledge and understanding of Eastern Orthodox monasticism by studying it directly in its purest form; and also to improve my knowledge and understanding of the traditional, liturgic arts of Orthodoxy by coming into direct contact with some of the finest examples of Byzantine architecture, painting, and music. What precisely are the aims of Athonite monasticism, and what are the means that are employed by the monks of Athos for achieving them? What is the relationship of these ends and means to the teaching of Christ, St. Paul, and the Eastern Christian Fathers? How are the monasteries and smaller monastic establishments on the Holy Mountain organized? What is the nature and extent of private prayer and common worship? What, besides these, constitutes the monks' daily round of activities? Is the ancient tradition of Eastern Orthodox mysticism, known as *hesychasm,* still alive on Athos? What books do the monks especially study and recommend? What are their views on monasticism, contemporary mankind, philosophy, solitude, hardship, fasting, prayer, etc.? What is the exact character of the architecture, painting, and music on Athos, and what part do these arts play in the life of the monks? These are some of the questions I sought to answer while visiting the Mountain, by observation and through numerous conversations with the monks.

My account, as I have indicated, is based on notes I took during my sojourns on Mount Athos. After leaving Athos, I worked over the notes, organizing the data and checking the dates of buildings, paintings, etc. in reliable works in the English and Greek languages. I have retained as far as possible the diary form, feeling that this has certain merits that would be lost if the material were to be worked over into a systematic treatise.

The third sojourn on the Mountain as well as the writing of the part of this work dealing with it (pp. 137-212) were made possible by a Fulbright Research grant, which enabled me to make a study of modern Greek thought while affiliated with the University of Athens during the academic years 1957-58 and 1958-59.

To render certain parts of the text clearer and more meaningful, I have employed many photographs and drawings, showing monasteries, churches, frescoes, panel icons, persons, and so on. Some of the photographs I took myself. A good number of them have been provided by Mr. Pericles Papachatzedakis, Athenian photographer, specifically, the ones that appear on pages 21, 64, 73, 85, 88, 94, 99, 102, 103, 120, 121, 132, 135, 150, 155 164. Those on pages 33, 38, and 39 have been provided by Mr. Fotis Zachariou, who has cleaned the frescoes shown. The drawings that appear on pages 27, 107, 159, 201, and 211, as well as some of the designs at the ends of chapters, have been done by Mr. Fotis Kontoglous. The rest have been drawn by his pupil Mr. Rallis Kopsidis. The diagram on p. 25, showing a typical Athonite main church, has been made by Professor Nicholas Moutsopoulos, of the University of Salonica,

In spelling Greek names and terms, I have in general endeavored to give phonetic equivalents of the modern Greek pronunciation, rather than to make simple orthographic transliterations.

I am deeply grateful to my brother, Professor John P. Cavarnos, of Austin College, Texas, and to Mr. Basil Laourdas, Director of the Institute for Balkan Studies at Salonica, for reading the entire manuscript and suggesting many improvements, and to Professor Michael Choukas, of Dartmouth College, and Professor Leslie Marchand, of Rutgers University, for reading major parts of the work and making valuable comments. I also owe thanks to Miss Elinor Rust for reading the proofs, and to Messrs. F. Kontoglous, R. Kopsidis, P. Papachatzedakis, F. Zachariou and N. Moutsopoulos for providing illustrations. Further, I am very grateful to the United States Educational Foundation in Greece, and to Mr. G. R. Hopwood, Executive Director, for assistance in the publication of this work.

CONSTANTINE CAVARNOS

University of Athens
May, 1959

CONTENTS

LIST OF ILLUSTRATIONS

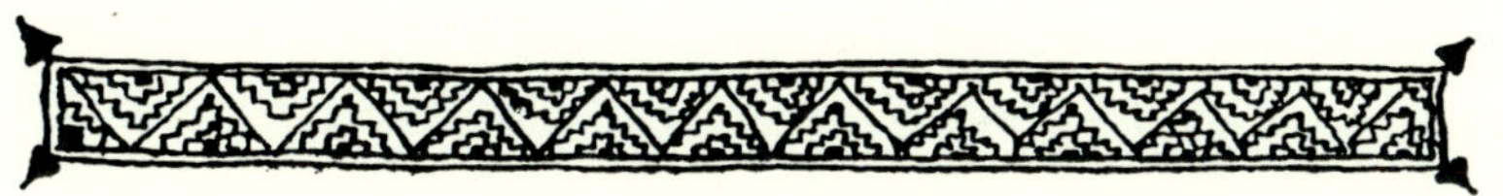

FROM SALONICA TO MOUNT ATHOS

Mount Athos or the Holy Mountain *(Aghion Oros)* may be reached from Salonica either by steamship or by motorboat, or one may travel part of the way by bus and the rest by motorboat. A small steamer, mainly a freighter, leaves Salonica, or «Thessaloniki,» for Mount Athos and other places every ten days; two good-sized motor launches sail for Athos once a week, on successive days; and buses leave for Ierissos, which is near Athos, daily. When I had decided to make the journey there in September, 1954, I inquired about all of these means and decided to take the bus to Ierissos and then make the rest of the journey by motorboat. If I were to have gone by steamship, I would have had to wait about a week for the arrival of the ship. If, on the other hand, I had chosen to go all the way by motor launch, I would have had to run the risk of an extended delay in some small harbor between Thessaloniki and Mount Athos due to motor trouble or rough seas.

I took with me only a brief case containing photographic equipment, and a cloth bag which I had used for my books while at college, with a few pieces of clothing, a notebook, and some other minor items. From my experience there in 1952, I realized that the less I took the better, because often the distance from one monastery to another has to be covered by foot, and this sometimes involves hours of walking on steep, rocky mule tracks. I considered even my shaving equipment an unnecessary burden and did not take it with me. What if I let my beard grow for a month or so, among people who have renounced shaving? I would feel more at home on Athos and would save an appreciable fraction of an hour every day that I could spend doing something more worthwhile!

The bus for Ierissos leaves Thessaloniki between seven and eight in the morning and arrives in Ierissos in about five hours. On the way there it passes through plains and villages that retain the fascinating contours, forms and atmosphere that they had hundreds of years ago, and over high mountains. It pauses for about half an hour in the town of Arnaia, where there are two restaurants, so that passengers who are to continue the journey may have lunch.

Ierissos is a small town that lies in a fertile plain close to the sea and the site of the ancient city of Acanthos. Its inhabitants are clean, industrious, peaceful people, who live by agriculture. Motorboats leave from here and from nearby Trypiti for Mount Athos only in the morning, and hence upon arriving in Ierissos I and a dozen or so other persons whose destination was Athos had to find some place to stay overnight. I proceeded to a small hotel named Acanthos, which is near the bus terminal.

After I had eaten at a little restaurant near the hotel, I walked down to the seashore and strolled back and forth, listening to the gentle, rhythmic sound of the waves that were rolling over the spotlessly clean sand of the beach. The sound was soothing and the fragrant air of the sea was invigorating.

From Ierissos one may take a motor launch to the Monastery of Vatopedi or to some other monastery on the northeast coast of the Athos peninsula, or he may take the bus to Trypiti, on the other side of the peninsula, and from there the motor launch to Daphne, the main port of Mount Athos. Usually the latter route is preferable, because frequently the sea on the northeast side is rough, whereas it tends to be fairly quiet on the southwest side. In either case, one has to spend a night in Ierissos or else in the nearby village of Nea Roda.

The bus left Ierissos at 6:30 in the morning and, after a brief stop in the village of Nea Roda, arrived at Try-

BEACH OF IERISSOS

piti, on the south side of the neck of the peninsula, in half an hour. Trypiti is not a town or village, but only a place having a wooden pier and a «coffee shop» *(kafeneio)*, where one may have light refreshments. The trip from Ierissos to Trypiti is mostly over flat land. In many places the land is quite close to the sea level, and some of the passengers who were familiar with this region, which is known as Provlakas (*pro*=before, *avlax*=canal), remarked that these were traces of the canal that had been cut in 480 B.C. by the Persian king Xerxes for the passage of his fleet.

When we arrived at Trypiti, the motorboat was ready to leave. The passengers proceeded at once to the pier and hopped in the boat, one after another. As soon as the baggage was in, the boat took off for Daphne, full of monks and laymen.

Two aspects of the thirty-five mile long peninsula are bound to impress the visitor greatly as the boat sails by it. One of these is the form of the Mountain, which rises abruptly and majestically near the outer extremity of the peninsula to a conical peak more than 6,400 feet above the sea. The other is the rich, deep green vegetation that covers the entire area, except for the soaring marble peak. Such vegetation—which consists of chestnut trees, firs, oaks, pines, poplars and other kinds of trees, and of many kinds of shrubs and herbs—is seldom seen in Greece. The abrupt terrain sets it off in relief and makes it a most beautiful and unforgettable sight. This vegetation is a great blessing to the monks: it not only provides for them an inspiring sight, but also constitutes their chief means of support. More than anything else, the money earned in the first place from the export of timber and in the next place from the export of hazelnuts, walnuts, and laurel oil, provides today the financial basis for the existence of the twenty monasteries of the Holy Mountain.

The boat arrived at Daphne at eleven o'clock, after having made a number of brief stops. Its first was at the village of Ouranoupolis, formerly called Prosphori or Pyrgos, which is situated by a Byzantine tower *(pyrgos)*, near the boundary wall that separates the neck of the Athos peninsula from the sacred territory. The remaining stops were at the *arsanades* of various monasteries. An *arsanas* here is a landing place, with warehouses and buildings for workers and seamen, and usually a tower, formerly used for defense against the pirates. Every monastery has its *arsanas*.

The port of Daphne, where I and most of the other passengers got off, is a small bay with a pier for motorboats and other small craft. The water of this bay is very deep, so that steamers are able to anchor not far from the pier.

There are about a dozen buildings in the vicinity of

DAPHNE

the landing place: a customhouse, a post office, a police station, a church, two restaurants, and several shops that sell groceries and hardware. The best supplied and most interesting store is that of Christos Theodorides, the boat agent. The majority of the laymen and monks who come to Daphne eat at this place, either in the narrow room at the rear or in the open space in front, under the trees. Here one will find among other things, various religious articles intended especially for visitors, such as little crucifixes, small icons carved in wood, rosaries made of various kinds of materials, and incense with a wonderful aroma. All the stores are operated by laymen—monks are not allowed to dwell in Daphne.

MONASTERY OF XEROPOTAMOU

From Daphne I set out for the Monastery of Xeropotamou, which is built on a plateau on the way to the village of Karyes, the capital of the Holy Mountain. In order for a visitor to be officially admitted into a monastery, he must present a *diamonitirion,* or letter from the Holy Board of Overseers at Karyes recommending him to the hospitality of the twenty monasteries. Without such a letter, one may be admitted into a monastery, with the understanding, however, that he will depart early the next day. My plan was to go to Xeropotamou, stay there overnight, and resume my journey to Karyes at dawn. Before beginning the difficult walk up the very steep path

MONASTERY OF XEROPOTAMOU

that leads from the coast to the monastery, I paused at a small beach some distance from Daphne and took a dip into the sea. The monks seldom go swimming, and when they do they go alone to out-of-the-way places; so I did likewise. The water was absolutely clear and of pleasant temperature.

Seen from Daphne, the Monastery of Xeropotamou appears to be only a short distance away. Actually it takes about three quarters of an hour to reach it by foot. Upon arriving, I explained to the gatekeeper *(portaris)* that I had come to Athos that day via Daphne and wished to see the monastery and, if possible, stay there overnight before proceeding to Karyes. He took me to the assistant guestmaster *(pararchondaris)* — the guestmaster *(archondaris)* himself was away — and explained my case. To my great pleasure, he told me that I could stay here until the next day, and without delay took me to a room in the guesthouse *(archondariki)* where I was to rest and sleep during my stay at the monastery. This room was clean, well-kept, furnished with a bed, a divan, a table, and a kerosene lamp. It should be noted that government officials, prelates, professors, scholars, and other «official» guests are given select private rooms, whereas «unofficial» guests are assigned to plain rooms with beds for several persons.

After I had rested a little, I went out to the courtyard to study the architecture and other features of the monastery. The courtyard is bounded by a square of four-storied buildings. The outer part of the quadrangle consists of tall, sturdy walls, and leaves only one entrance. At the highest corner of the quadrangle there is a tall tower of defense.

Standing free at the center of Xeropotamou's courtyard is the main church, known as the *katholikon.* It is a large structure with seven domes: three over the esonarthex, which is known on Athos as the *liti* — a big one at the center, and two smaller ones on either side, at northwest and southwest angles of it; three small ones over the sanctuary *(bema)* — two over the side apses and one, set at a higher level, over the central apse; and one, by far the largest and set at the highest level, over the nave. The church's interior far surpasses the exterior in beauty and grandeur. The floor is paved with large marble slabs, while the walls are decorated with frescoes. In the central dome, looking down, is a fresco depicting Christ as Pantocrator, «Ruler of All.» Hanging down from the intersection point of two iron bars that are fastened to the lower part of the drum and form a cross is a large chandelier, and around it is a beautiful *choros* or corona — a very large, circular, brass chandelier with loosely fitted joints, held by twelve chains that are fastened to the lower part of the drum. The *katholikon* of every Athonite monastery has such a *choros.* At the top of the iconostasis, above the Beautiful or Holy Gate — the door at the middle of iconostasis — is a big crucifix. This crucifix serves as a vivid reminder to the monks of Christ's statement: «If any man will come after me, let him deny himself, and take up his cross, and follow me» (Luke 9: 23); and of Paul's: «Those who belong to Christ Jesus have crucified the flesh with its passions and desires» (Gal. 5: 24), and «the world is crucified unto me, and I unto the world» (Gal. 6: 14).

Although Xeropotamou was founded centuries earlier, the present *katholikon* was built in 1761 and was frescoed in 1783. One of the monks told me that the old *katholikon* was torn down and was replaced by this one because it was too small to accommodate all the monks. Today there are only thirty monks here, but judging from the number of cells, there must have been at one time as many as two or three hundred.

At this as at the other monasteries of the Holy Mountain, there is daily an *orthros* (matins), a liturgy, and a

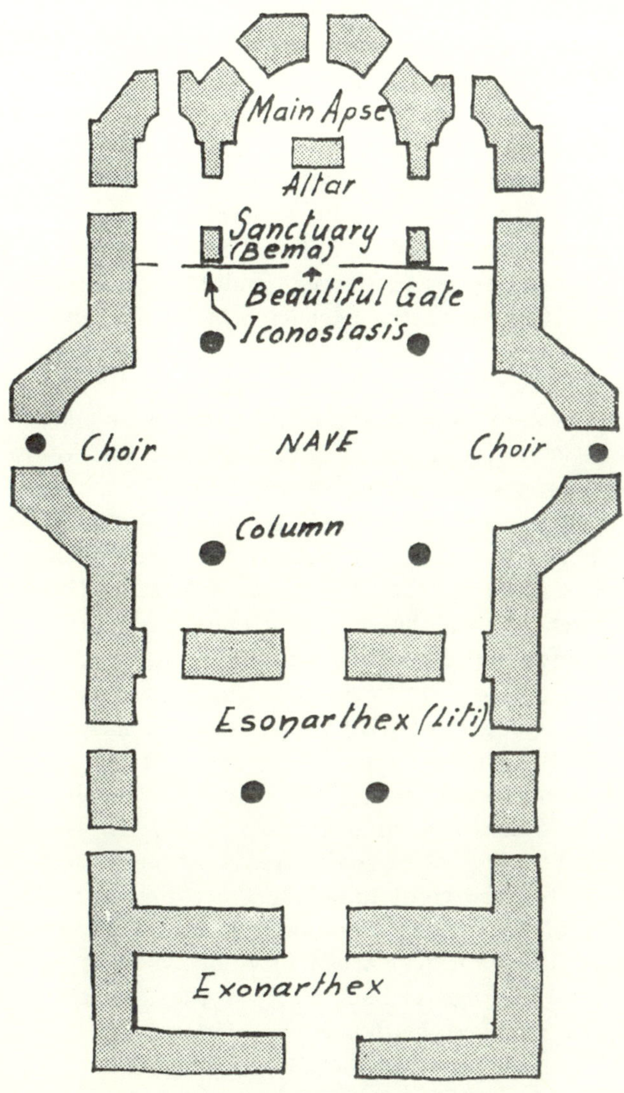

PLAN OF TYPICAL ATHONITE KATHOLIKON

vesper service. The first of these is preceded by an hour of private prayer, known as *kanonas*. On the day of my arrival the vespers started well before sunset and took about three quarters of an hour. The *orthros*, the next day, started about half past two in the morning, according to our time system, and was followed immediately by the liturgy. The two together lasted about four hours.

It should be noted that in determining the time for their church services and other activities the Holy Community, which resides in Karyes, and all the monasteries on Mount Athos, with the exception of Iviron and Vatopedi, follow the Byzantine time system. The basis of this time system is sunset: when the sun sets, it is twelve o'clock; the hour immediately after is one o'clock, the next hour is two, and so on. Iviron is unique in following the Chaldean system, taking sunrise instead of sunset for twelve o'clock, while Vatopedi has adopted the Western time system. Sunrise and sunset are relative to the peak of Athos: sunrise is when the first rays strike the peak, while sunset is when the last rays leave it. This system obviously invovles clock-shifting to fit the seasons, but has the advantage of following the rhythm of nature.

Xeropotamou is *idiorrhythmic*. This means, for one thing, that the monks do not eat together in the refectory, but each prepares and eats his food in his own cell, at such times as he wants, following his own (*idios*) «rhythm», except on certain special or major feasts. It means also that each monk has the right to hold private property. In an idiorrhythmic monastery the monks are allotted every so often a certain quantity of bread, olive-oil, vegetables, wine, etc.; but such things as fish, meat, clothes, and stationery are not provided by the monastery—the monks buy these from the small amount of money allotted to them at certain intervals. Further, an idiorrhythmic monastery does not have an abbot (*igoumenos*), but has a committee of two

CHRIST THE PANTOCRATOR

or three senior monks, known as *epitropoi,* who are elected annually from among the *proïstamenoi,* the five or fifteen leading monks of the monastery. Together with the *proïstamenoi,* they constitute the *synaxis,* or assembly. The *epitropoi* are the executive part of the *synaxis* and also the spiritual authority of the brotherhood. In a coenobitic monastery, on the other hand, the monks eat together, in the refectory, all property is held in common, and the community is governed by an abbot assisted by a committee of two or three senior monks (*epitropoi*). In very important administrative matters the abbot must consult the *gerontia,* or board of elders, consisting of eight to ten senior monks. His spiritual authority, however, he exercises alone, without the *epitropoi* or the *gerontia.* He is elected for life by those members of the monastery who have been monks for at least six years, whereas the membership of the committee of *epitropoi* changes every year. Of the two systems, the coenobitic is the older and more austere. This system is based on the rules that were formulated by the saints Pachomios (292-346), Basil the Great (329-379), Theodore the Studite (759-826), and Athanasios the Athonite (ca. 920-1003), whereas the idiorrhythmic system appears towards the end of the fourteenth century and becomes more prevalent in the fifteenth and sixteenth centuries. At the present time eleven of the monasteries on Mount Athos are coenobitic and nine are idiorrhythmic.

On the day when I arrived at Xeropotamou, the Decapitation of St. John the Baptist was being commemorated and a fast was observed. A fast on Mount Athos does not mean simply that one abstains from meat, nor does it mean that one abstains from food altogether. It means abstinence not only from meat, which though permitted in the idiorrhythmic monasteries is seldom eaten and is altogether excluded in the coenobitic monasteries and in the sketes, but also abstinence from fresh fish — dried or salted fish are sometimes eaten — as well as from eggs, cheese and other items of animal origin, and even from oil and wine. About two-thirds of the days of the year are days of fasting: Lent and several other long periods of fasting, every Wednesday and Friday — and in the case of the coenobitic monasteries, every Monday as well — throughout the year, and the day that precedes every notable holy day. Visitors and workmen normally have to observe the fasts, but not with the same strictness as the monks, except those of Lent and the fortnight before the feast of the Dormition of the Virgin Mary on August 15th.

Regarding the practice of fasting on Monday, Wednesday, and Friday, Callistos and Ignatios Xanthopoulos, who led a monastic life on Mount Athos during the fourteenth century, say: «Three days a week, that is, on Monday, Wednesday, and Friday, eat only once a day, partaking of six ounces of bread, and of dry food not to satiation, and of water up to three or four cups, if you want, following the 69th rule of the Holy Apostles, which says: If a bishop, or a priest, or a deacon, or a reader, or a chanter does not fast during the holy Forty Days before Easter, or on Wednesday or Friday, let him be cast out, unless he does this because of bodily illness; if he be a layman, let him be excommunicated. Fast on Monday was instituted later by the holy Fathers (*Philokalia,* Athens, 1893, Vol. 2, p. 370).

Fasting takes into account both the quantity and the quality of food. The idea is to eat a smaller amount of food during a fasting day; to abstain from fats and oils, as these tend to fatten the body and thereby arouse lust and make one physically and spiritually lazy; to abstain from meat, fish, and products of animal origin, as these tend to excite carnal desire; and also to abstain from mere delicacies, as the consumption of these is a form of self-indulgence. St. John Climacos (c. 525-605) says: «Satiety of food is a begetter of unchastity.» He also says: «Let us cut down fatty and greasy foods, foods that inflame carnal desire, and foods that sweeten and tickle the larynx» (*The Ladder,* Migne, *P.G.,* 88, 864, 865).

The practice of fasting is not regarded as an end in itself, as something having intrinsic value, but only as a means, as a necessary condition for the spiritual life. It belongs to the category of what the Eastern, Byzantine Fathers call «bodily virtues,» among which are prostrations, standing, and vigils. Referring to these, St. John Damascene (c. 676-c. 754) says that they «are rather instruments for the virtues; they are necessary, if one practices them with humility and spiritual knowledge. For without them neither do the virtues of the soul come into being, but in themselves they are of no benefit, any more than plants without fruit» (*Philokalia,* 2, 17). And St. Gregory the Sinaite (1289-1360), speaking specifically of fasting, observes: «Constant fasting withers lust and gives birth to self-restraint» (*Philokalia,* 2, 272); while Callistos and Ignatios Xanthopoulos remark: «Fasting and self-restraint are the first virtue, the mother, root, source and foundation of all good» (*Philokalia,* 2, 370).

KARYES

Early in the morning of my second day on Athos, I set out for Karyes, having as my guide a middle-aged laborer who was going there on an errand for Xeropotamou. It took us an hour and three quarters of almost uninterrupted walking at a moderate pace to reach Karyes. The path that leads there is uphill most of the way.

KARYES

A solemn silence prevails at this village, as elsewhere on the Holy Mountain. There are no automobiles or carts on its clean, stone-paved streets, no phonographs or radios in the shops, no children at play, no dogs to bark. Singing, whistling, and shouting are forbidden. The playing and even the possession of musical instruments of any kind whatsoever is forbidden here and everywhere else on Athos. No women are to be seen, as they are not allowed to set foot anywhere on the peninsula beyond the boundary wall.

Not only noise and secular and instrumental music, but also smoking is considered irreverent, and is forbidden in the streets of Karyes and in the courtyards of the monasteries. «The fumes of tobacco,» I have heard a monk say, «are the incense of the Devil.» This should not be taken to mean that no Athonite monk smokes. But the practice among the monks is rare. At some of the monasteries, such as Dionysiou, the monks are absolutely forbidden to smoke, and certain monks, known as «zealots,» abhor the practice. St. Nicodemos the Aghiorite (1749-1809), whose writings are highly esteemed by the monks of Athos, particularly the zealots, has devoted a special section of his *Manual of Counsel (Symvouleftikon Encheiridion)* to a condemnation of smoking. He regards it as especially unbecoming to the clergy, because it is opposed not only to the health of the body but also to morality, being very «loathsome, abominable, and vulgar» (1885, p. 57).

Upon arriving, I went and had breakfast at a small inn operated by a layman. Later, I visited various stores run by monks: a bookstore, a shoemaker's shop, a grocery, and two souvenir shops which sell beautiful carved woodwork—crosses, icons, seals, cups, forks, spoons — made by Athonite hermits, and also frankincense, rosaries, and other religious articles.

In order to procure an official letter of admission to the twenty monasteries, I went to the police station and presented the letters of introduction that I had gotten from the Greek Ministries of Education and Foreign Affairs, and received a note. Then I proceeded to the building of the *Iera Koinotis,* the Holy Community, and presented this

THE RESURRECTION
Detail showing St. John the Baptist, Adam and Eve, and Abel. Fresco, Church of the Protaton

together with the letters and my passport to one of the ushers *(seïmenides)* of the *Koinotis*. Soon a form was filled out by the chief secretary and was signed by the four members of the *Iera Epistasia,* the Holy Board of Overseers, and stamped by a seal made up of four parts, corresponding to the four monks who constitute the *Epistasia*. This paper was my letter of admission to the monasteries.

What exactly are the *Koinotis* and the *Epistasia?* The *Koinotis* is the central governing body of the Holy Mountain, and consists of twenty monks, one from each monastery, who reside in Karyes and assemble regularly every Monday and Friday—except during Lent, when they meet on Tuesdays and Thursdays—and at other times when necessary. These monks are elected annually, between the first and the tenth of January, each monastery electing its own representative. The *Epistasia* is the executive part of the *Koinotis,* and consists of four members, called *epistatai*. These remain in power for a year and are succeeded by four other *epistatai,* and these by four others the year after, and so on, until the representative of every monastery has served in turn. This means that for administrative purposes the twenty monasteries have been divided into five groups of four, and that each of these groups exercises the executive duties for a year every five years.

In addition to the central governing body, which is made up of monks, there is a civil governor *(dioikitis),* who is appointed by the Greek Ministry of Foreign Affairs, and who sees to it that there are no violations of the Constitutional Charter of Mount Athos and that public order and security are maintained. The policemen who are stationed on Athos are under his direct orders. As far as spiritual and ecclesiastical matters are concerned, the Holy Mountain is directly subject to the Ecumenical Patriarchate.

Across from the building of the Holy Community, only a few steps away, is the most important church on Athos,

THE EVANGELIST LUKE
Fresco, Church of the Protaton

belonging to all the Athonite monasteries — the Church of the Protaton. This church dates from 965, and is a basilica, the only main church of that type on the Holy Mountain.

The exterior of this edifice, which has recently been extensively repaired, is very simple, yet majestic. The ground plan is oblong. The side walls are perforated with tall round arched windows, while those of the clerestory are pierced by similar small ones. The building leans over to the north side, and buttresses have been constructed on that side to carry the outward thrust. The interior has the form of a cross, which has been achieved by dividing the church — not including the narthex — from the east to the west into three oblong sections, a broad one at the middle and a narrow one on each side, and cutting the side sections at the ends by means of walls, thus forming rectangular divisions at each end. The eastern arm of the cross is separated from the rest by the iconostasis.

CHURCH OF THE PROTATON

When one enters the Church of the Protaton, he is impressed by its length and height and by the superb frescoes that adorn its walls. All the walls, except those of the narthex, which appears to have been constructed or reconstructed at a later date, are decorated with frescoes that were painted at the beginning of the fourteenth century by one of the greatest masters of Byzantine iconography, Manuel Panselinos of Thessaloniki. No description, even the most detailed and most eloquent, can give one an adequate idea of the beauty and power of these icons. I had read about them and discussed them with men who had spent months studying and copying them in this very building, but I was never able to imagine anything so sublime. These representations of sacred persons and incidents are not naturalistic, as some have asserted; nor are they products of man's arbitrary imagination. They are the forms of new, transfigured men, impressed upon matter by an artist who succeeded in rising above the realm of nature and the realm of the imagination to that of the spirit.

What impressed me most of all as I gazed at the figures depicted on the walls was the quality perhaps best described by the term spiritual grandeur. Their postures, gestures, and above their faces express this quality in a striking manner: they express great seriousness of character, freedom from all pretense and servility, and great spiritual depth. Surrounded by these figures, one feels that he is in the presence not merely of paintings, but of beings far more real than persons that he meets in everyday life. These sacred figures bear the clear impress of complete self-mastery, inner unity, and freedom from everything petty, from all impatience and weakness. Everything about them bespeaks great calm and tremendous inner power. The contemplation of these icons introduces one into a new dimension of being. It makes one experience these sublime qualities, arouses one's admiration for them, and awakens and strengthens the desire to acquire them.

The traditional means of attracting the attention of the beholder to the face, where these qualities are especially expressed, have been employed with exceptional skill by Panselinos. Thus, the halo that surrounds the head has been made very large and has been set in bold relief by

ST. PROCOPIOS
Fresco, Church of the Protaton

ST. THEODORE
Fresco, Church of the Protaton

painting around it a red and then a white band, and setting the whole in a dark blue background.

As far as the colors are concerned, I noted also the following. They are beautiful, but not loud. Sometimes they show a striking disregard for nature. For example, a greenish hue has been used a great deal on the faces and other exposed parts of the body, especially at the edges. There is a large variety of colors, many of which are light. Blue has been employed frequently and extensively. Thus, the garments of many figures are blue, and the background is always dark blue. White also has been used very much, sometimes all by itself; sometimes in conjunction with black or brown: for instance, in the case of the garments of the Great Hierarchs (St. John Chrysostom, St. Gregory the Theologian, etc.) black and white, and brown and white have been employed to form a contrasted pattern of crosses; and frequently, in combination with other colors to form light hues, such as light green, light red, and light brown. In the representation of certain saints, such as St. Paul and the Athonite hermits, a simple combination of colors has been employed, whereas a greater variety of colors and much ornamentation has been used in the representation of the Hebrew and Christian king-saints.

The bodily form of the older figures differs markedly from that of the younger ones: the face and body of Christ and other young figures are full, whereas the faces of the older saints, especially of the Athonite hermits, are thin, the cheeks sunken, and the bodies slender or even emaciated. But all the figures are large, so that even those on the uppermost of the four strips of frescoes that cover the walls of the church can be seen very distinctly by anyone with normal vision. These paintings were clearly meant to be, not merely ornamental, but *liturgic,* that is, to be seen in all their details and to evoke religious experience.

Fotis Zachariou, the artist and restorer who was sent

ST. EUTHYMIOS THE GREAT
Fresco, Church of the Protaton

to Athos a few years ago by the Greek Ministry of Education and Religion to clean these murals, has done an excellent job. Those that are very well preserved look as if they had just been done. Zachariou has avoided retouching the frescoes or repainting damaged areas, considering such a thing undesirable, as it involves the danger of altering or distorting the paintings. Thus the beholder has the satisfaction of knowing that what he sees is wholly the work of the original artist.

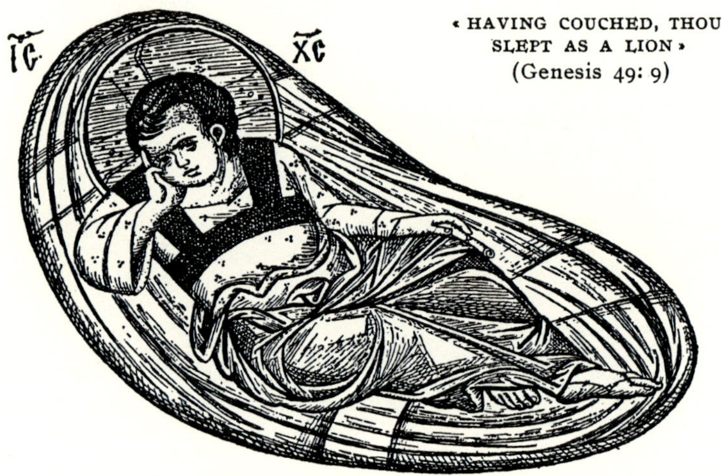

« HAVING COUCHED, THOU SLEPT AS A LION »
(Genesis 49: 9)

THE CHILD CHRIST RECLINING
Fresco, Church of the Protaton

MONASTERY OF KOUTLOUMOUSIOU

Lying in a valley, only ten minutes from the Protaton, is the coenobitic Monastery of Koutloumousiou, which was founded towards the end of the thirteenth century. It has twenty monks and five novices. Of the twenty monks,

MONASTERY OF KOUTLOUMOUSIOU

five are active, performing various tasks and taking part in the church services. Another five, very old and in poor health, stay in the monastery's hospital, while the rest, also far advanced in years, remain in the section for the aged.

As the monastery is coenobitic, the monks have their meals together, in the refectory, which is west of the main church. I was invited to eat with them. The meals are always preceded and followed by a brief prayer. During the meal, one of the monks reads from a holy book. He stands up and reads in a slow, clear, loud voice, so that every word can be heard distinctly.

The practice of reading during the meals serves a number of purposes. It provides good training for the younger monks, who are usually appointed for this task; it eliminates all talking and thus makes it possible for the monks to masticate their food better; and it raises eating from the merely biological to the spiritual plane, by providing food for the soul. Referring to this practice, St. Basil the Great, one of the founders of Orthodox monasticism, says in his *Shorter Rules* that monks ought to listen to such reading «with far greater pleasure than they eat and drink, in order that the mind may be shown not to be distracted by the pleasures of the body, but delighting rather in the words of the Lord....» And St. Ephraim the Syrian, who was a contemporary of St. Basil, says: «When the body is hungry and demands food, then remember that the soul, too, asks for its own proper food. And just as the body cannot live if it does not receive bread, so also the soul is dead if it is not nourished by means of spiritual wisdom. For man is dual, made up of soul and body, and this is why the Savior said that man shall not live by bread alone» (*Ascetic Works,* edited by M. D. Sakorraphos, Athens, 1864, p. 28).

Among the monks with whom I had occasion to talk a good deal was Maximos, the librarian *(bibliothekarios)*. Father Maximos took me to the library, which consists of two moderately sized rooms containing about seven hundred fifty manuscripts and a much larger number of printed books, kept in glass-doored cases. Both in the library and in the courtyard we discussed the practices of Athonite monks, particularly mental prayer *(noera prosefhi)* or prayer of the heart *(kardiaki prosefhi)*. This form of prayer is described as follows by Nikephoros the Solitary (died c. 1340), one of the great ascetics of Mount Athos: «You know that the seat of thoughts of every man is in the breast, for when the lips are silent it is here that we talk and deliberate and recite our prayers and psalms and so on. Therefore, having banished every thought from the discursive faculty — you can do this if you want to — give it this prayer: ‹Lord Jesus Christ, Son of God, have mercy upon me.› And force this instead of any other thought always to cry within. If you keep this up for a time, the way to the heart will be opened by it» (*Philokalia,* 2, 241). Another outstanding Athonite monk, Nicodemos, gives this description: «Mental prayer, or prayer of the heart, according to the Holy Fathers known as Vigilant *(Niptikoi)*, is chiefly this: that a man gather his mind in his heart and, without speaking with his mouth, solely with the word residing in his mind which speaks in the heart, say the following brief prayer: ‹Lord Jesus Christ, Son of God, have mercy upon me,› holding his breath a little» *(O Aoratos Polemos — The Unseen Warfare,* Athens, 1947, p. 147). Maximos was surprised to find that I, who lived in «the world,» was interested in such a practice, which is so remote from the materialism of our age. But seeing that I was genuinely interested in the subject, he expressed himself more freely. He showed me a copy of the *Philokalia,* which he asserted contains a great deal on this subject, and said that he had a copy of this work in his room and studied it. (The *Philokalia* is a monumental work containing writings by many Eastern Orthodox ascetics and mystics, rang-ing from the fourth to the fifteenth century. It was compiled by St. Macarios Notaras (1731-1805), Archbishop of Corinth, and St. Nicodemos the Aghiorite, and was first published in 1782. Parts of this work, translated into English from the Russian version of the Greek original, were published in England in 1951 in a volume entitled *Writings from the Philokalia on Prayer of the Heart,* and in 1954 in a volume entitled *Early Fathers from the Philokalia.*) Maximos also showed me a copy of *Evergetinos,* and remarked that this is another excellent book to read on the subject. (*Evergetinos* consists of a collection of excerpts from the works of numerous Eastern Fathers arranged under various headings. It was compiled by a monk named Paul and known as Evergetinos, and was first published in 1783. The actual title of the work is: *Collection of Sayings and Teachings of God-inspired and Holy Fathers.*)

«*Evergetinos,*» said Maximos, «constitutes good preparation for the *Philokalia.* The little book entitled *The Adventures of a Pilgrim (Oi Peripeteies enos Proskynitou)* also is very helpful. This work was written by a Russian reader of the *Philokalia,* apparently about the middle of the nineteenth century, and was published in Russia in 1884, after the manuscript was found on Athos. It is a wonderful book. I have read it over a hundred times.»

(An English translation of the last named work, entitled *The Way of a Pilgrim,* was published in 1930, 1941, and 1952.)

Maximos believes that the great decline in spirituality in our time has made the practice of mental prayer almost totally incomprehensible, not only to those who live in the world, but even to most monks.

«But there are signs,» he remarked, «that people are beginning to return to Christianity and are becoming interested in this and similar subjects. An appreciable number of visitors to our monastery — Germans, French, Amer-

THE CRUCIFIXION
Fresco, katholikon of Koutloumousiou

icans, Greeks, and so on — ask especially for works of the hesychasts [Byzantine mystics], such as St. Symeon the New Theologian, St. Gregory of Sinai, St. Gregory Palamas, and others.

«As far as the monastic life is concerned,» he went

on, «in spite of its present decline, the fact remains that mental prayer, or prayer of the heart, as well as other practices, such as strict and regular fasting, can be followed most easily and successfully only in monastic communities of the sort that survive on Mount Athos, where solitude, quietness, and other essential conditions are provided. Mental prayer is the highest form of spiritual striving, and calls for great efforts, contempt of all earthly things, and living in quietness in one place.»

«Is it possible,» I asked, «to practice this prayer durring church services, which take up so much of the monk's time?»

«Yes,» replied Maximos. «One can carry on simultaneously two or even three different activities: one can listen to the chanting or the reading, following what is said, and also pray mentally. In the refectory, a monk can simultaneously eat, listen to the reading, and pray. Repeated prayer of the heart increases one's ability to do this. To get important results, one must practice this form of prayer with single-mindedness over a long period.»

From my talks with Maximos I was able to gather the following information about him. He is in his seventies and has been a monk for over thirty years. Before he became a monk, he was a businessman. In his spare time he used to read a great deal on spiritualism, reincarnation, and the like, because he was thirsty for the truth. But he found that such writings instead of clearing up things for him made him more and more confused. So he stopped reading them. Finally, he gave up everything and withdrew to the monastery.

«As a result of living the monastic life,» he said, «I have been finding more and more of the truth.»

Maximos has cut all contact with the world. He doesn't even correspond with anyone, and refuses to tell people what part of Greece he is from.

«They write me,» he said, «but I never reply to anyone.»

In spite of his age, he is upright, healthy-looking, agile, and alert.

The most outstanding among the novices *(dokimoi monachoi)* at Koutloumousiou is a tall, slim, bright-eyed youth, not yet twenty, who is a student at the Athonias School, near Karyes. What is his past? How does he like Mount Athos? Will he stay here? These were some of the questions I put to him.

«I was in an orphanage before I came here,» he replied. «Both my mother and my father are dead. Life here is much more interesting than at the orphanage, where I was for six years. I like monastic life and I enjoy my studies. I certainly intend to stay here.»

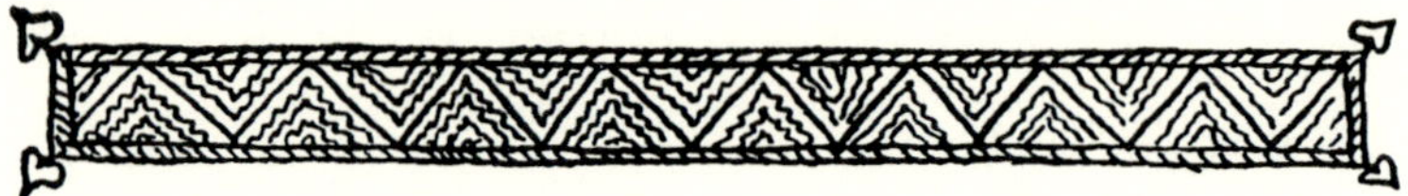

KELLI OF THE HOLY APOSTLES

A short distance from Koutloumousiou is the Kelli of the Holy Apostles, which is a dependency of this monastery. The term *kelli* as used here denotes a monastic establishment consisting of a building with a chapel in it and some surrounding land, and usually inhabited by three monks. There are about two hundred *kellia* on the Holy Mountain. The Kelli of the Holy Apostles is inhabited by half a dozen monks, headed by a young Cretan priest-monk named Eugene. Father Eugene is a graduate of the Theological School of the University of Thessaloniki and was for a time the chief assistant of the bishop of Kilkis.

I met Eugene at the Monastery of Koutloumousiou, and he invited me to visit his *kelli*. We went there together, and he showed me the garden, some ancient walls, and two remnants of very old and remarkable frescoes, one of them depicting the head of the Child Christ and the other the head of St. Panteleïmon. The style of these paintings is similar to that of Panselinos.

«These frescoes,» said Eugene, «were found in the old church whose ruins survive in our basement. Long ago, there stood at this site the Monastery of Alypiou. This is testified by the remains of sturdy walls which you see here and by certain documents that I have been studying. Some day I hope to piece together the history of the ancient monastery.»

The *kelli* was uninhabited, abandoned for years, when

Eugene took it over. Soon he transformed it into a place of active monastic life. He repaired the building, equipped it with furniture, brought monks, cultivated the land, and installed an old olive press as well as a motor which operates a flour mill and a saw for cutting and trimming lumber.

RUSSIAN SKETE OF ST. ANDREW

From the Kelli of the Holy Apostles I went to the Seraï, the «Palace,» a few minutes north of Karyes. The Seraï is a monastic dependency of the type known as a *skete*. There are twelve sketes on the Holy Mountain, four coenobitic and eight idiorrhythmic. Of the coenobitic sketes two are Russian, one is Bulgarian, and one Rumanian, while of the idiorrhythmic seven are Greek and one is Rumanian. The Seraï is a coenobitic Russian skete dedicated to the Apostle St. Andrew. An idiorrhythmic skete looks like a sparsely populated village. It consists of a group of small houses inhabited by hermits and having a common church, called the *kyriakon*. A coenobitic skete, on the other hand, is to all appearances a monastery, consisting of a quadrangle of buildings with a main church in the courtyard. The Skete of St. Andrew looks like a large monastery, consisting of a quadrangle of imposing buildings with a very large main church in the courtyard. This skete was founded by the Russians in the middle of the last century, and attemps were made by them to secure for it the status of a monastery, but failed. The Seraï has remained a dependency of the Monastery of Vatopedi.

At one time there lived here as many as six hundred monks. Now the skete is in a serious state of decline. Apart from the Athonias Ecclesiastic School, which is housed here, there are few signs of life. Only an occasional aged monk is to be seen, going quietly about his tasks, ignoring visitors. There are nineteen monks altogether — eighteen Russians and a Greek, who serves as secretary.

The main church of the Seraï is the largest church on the Holy Mountain and one of the most impressive. It is a modern structure, which has been aptly characterized by Archimandrite Gabriel, abbot of the Monastery of Dionysiou, as having «everything in it glittering and sumptuous, but bulky and heavy, evoking astonishment and admiration instead of the contrition that one experiences in churches of the Byzantine order» (*Lausaïkon tou Aghiou Orous—Lausaïkon of the Holy Mountain,* Volos, 1953, p. 59).

Concerning the Ecclesiastical School, I should note the following. It is housed in a large, four-storied building that was formerly used by the Russians as a guesthouse. It has six grades. During the first three, various high school courses are taught, with emphasis on ancient and modern Greek. The fourth year is devoted equally to classical Greek literature and to theology, while the last two years are devoted exclusively to theology. Having been reestablished in 1953, after a long interruption — since 1940 — caused by the Second World War, the school is on an experimental basis. In order to be admitted, one must pass certain entrance examinations. Only monks or persons who intend to become monks and are over sixteen years of age are accepted. Laymen who do not become monks at the end of their third year of study are required to leave the school. The expenses of the students and the rent for the building are paid by the Holy Community. The faculty members, eight in number, are all laymen, and are appointed and paid by the Greek Ministry of Education and Religion. The Dean, Nathaniel of the Monastery of Lavra, has been appointed by the Ecumenical Patriarchate.

MOLYVOCCLESIA

Northwest of Karyes, about half an hour from the Skete of St. Andrew, is Molyvocclesia, a *kelli* that belongs to the Serbian Monastery of Hilandari. (Of the twenty monasteries on Athos, seventeen are Greek, one is Bulgar-

ST. ANDREW OF CRETE AND ST. GREGORY OF GREATER ARMENIA
Frescoes, Chapel of Molyvocclesia

ian, one Russian, and one Serbian.) I visited this *kelli* in order to see its remarkable frescoes.

When I arrived, I found only one monk, busy making

a beehive. I greeted him with the customary Athonite *Evlogite,* «Give your blessing,» to which he replied, similarly in the Athonite manner, *O Kyrios,* «The Lord» — that is, «May the Lord bless you.» He was a Greek. I asked him if he resided here all alone, and he answered that he lived with two other monks, both of them Greeks, and explained that they were away at the time, having gone to one of the estates of the *kelli* to pick up the olives that had fallen to the ground.

Upon learning why I had come, he stopped his work and led me into the house. This building has a large reception room, a storeroom, a kitchen, bedrooms for the monks, and a small chapel, which is downstairs. I was taken to chapel to pray, and then we went upstairs again, to the reception room. The monk now served me some preserve made of watermelon peel, a tiny cup of coffee, and a glass of water.

During our conversation, this courteous monk, who came to the Mountain from a village of the Halkidiki when he was ten years old, and has remained here ever since for forty-five years, expressed sorrow that Athos is becoming depopulated, because people have become indifferent or even hostile to monasticism, forgetting the priceless contributions it has made to mankind through the centuries.

After our talk, I went to the church again to study and photograph the frescoes that adorn its whole interior. Although they were done more than four centuries ago (1537), they are very well preserved. These paintings belong to the Cretan School of iconography, which is characterized by tall, narrow forms, and closely repeated folds of the garments. Great seriousness and spirituality are imprinted on the faces of the saints, recalling in this respect the works of Panselinos, the supreme master of the other school of Athonite iconography, the Macedonian.

The effect produced by the contemplation of these figures in such a little church, where they are close to the beholder on all sides, is very powerful. Even one who has never experienced humility, contrition, and similar feelings will probably to some degree be aroused to the experience of such feelings when he contemplates these sacred paintings.

MONASTERY OF IVIRON

My next stopping place was the Monastery of Iviron, on the northeastern side of the Athos peninsula. Iviron is built a short distance from the sea, on a small plain, and is reached from Karyes by a stone-paved path that goes downhill for the most part. I made the journey alone, and met no one during my hour and a half walk. When I arrived at this ancient monastery—it was founded in 980—I felt relieved to find the gate open, as I had left Karyes late in the afternoon and there was some chance of my arriving at Iviron too late to be admitted inside. The gate of Athonite monasteries closes at about sunset, and if one arrives after the gate has been closed, he has to stay outside until the next day.

Supper was served to me and other laymen in the dining room of the guesthouse. The meal consisted of boiled rice, spaghetti with tomato sauce, whole wheat bread, wine, and water. Shortly after supper, each one retired to his room. The beds in the guest rooms are quite in keeping with the austere spirit of Athonite monasticism: the mattresses are set on unyielding boards.

The next day, breakfast was brought to my room by the assistant guestmaster. It consisted of a little cup of coffee and a glass of water. Lunch and supper were served in the dining room of the guesthouse. I had these in the company of three students of the University of Athens who had been sent here by the Greek Archeological Service, of the Ministry of Education and Religion, to classify

ARSANAS OF IVIRON

the books and make a file system that would include all the manuscripts and printed books of the monastery.

These young men informed me that there are here close to fourteen hundred manuscripts and about fifteen thousand printed books, among which are numerous first editions of important works. Most of the books, they told me, are Greek, while the rest are Latin, Slavic, Russian, and French. This library is one of the largest and most important on Mount Athos.

The librarian is an elderly priest-monk named Athanasios. He is tall, vigorous looking, upright, of austere and impressive mien, strong character, and keen intellect. He speaks French fluently, and occasionally reads French authors such as Victor Hugo. I had the pleasure of conversing with him a number of times. On one occasion, as we were sitting outside a chapel in the spacious quadrangular courtyard, our talk turned to the questions of God, creation, man's nature and destiny. Father Athanasios argued that:

«Neither science nor man's earthly life make sense, unless there is a Creator and Ruler of the universe, and an afterlife. Everything points to the existence of God and the reality of a life beyond this.»

He made reference to recent physical and astronomical theories, and quoted statements made by philosophers and theologians.

Athanasios is probably the most noteworthy figure among the fifty monks that live in this monastery. There is no abbot, as the monastery is idiorrhythmic.

At one time, Iviron possessed great wealth; now it is in financial difficulties, having suffered among other losses the destruction by fire of the greater part of its forest during the war against the communists. Before the Second World War, it had electric lighting—it is the only monastery on Athos besides Vatopedi and Hilandari that ever had electricity. Now the generator is unserviceable and lighting is provided by kerosene lamps. In spite of its poverty, however, Iviron is pervaded throughout by an air of ancient dignity. Its buildings are large and majestic, and quiet reigns in them and in the courtyard at all times, both day and night, broken only by the sounds of the bells and the iron or wooden gong, the *semantron,* that summon the monks to the church services. This quiet brought to my mind the Patristic teaching that God is peace, beyond noise and agitation, and that those who wish to know Him must be in a state of peace.

During my stay at Iviron, the *semantron* sounded for matins at 3:15. Liturgy immediately followed this service and ended at 6:15. At Iviron and at all the other Athonite monasteries, the first of these services is held regularly in the *katholikon,* while the second is performed in one of the chapels, except on Sundays and festivals, when it takes place in the main church.

While the services are going on, the monks stand in the stalls *(stasidia),* which are ranged along the walls. They wear their tall, black, cylindrical hats known as *skoufoi,* removing them only at certain points of the liturgy, as when the chanter sings: «Let us put away all worldly care, so that we may receive the King of all, invisibly escorted by the angelic Hosts,» and the Entry of the Holy Gifts takes place; and when the priest says: «Thine own of Thine own we offer to Thee, in all and for all;» and again when he says: «With the fear of God, with faith and love draw near.» At such times the monks descend from the low wooden platform on which the stalls are set, take off their hats, and stand with their heads bowed. They do not kneel. The practice of kneeling when the priest says: «Thine own of Thine own we offer to Thee...,» which is observed in Greek Orthodox churches in America and in some city churches in Greece, is an innovation, probably taken over from the Russians.

When the service is approaching the end, the monks descend from the platform of the stalls one at a time, approach the iconostasis and kiss the icons. They start with the icon of Christ, which is to the right (south) of the Beautiful Gate, cross themselves before it and kiss it, and then kiss in succession the other icons on this side of the iconostasis. Then they do the same thing on the left side of the iconostasis, starting with the icon of the Holy

ST. PETER
Panel icon, XVIIth century
Chapel of St. John the Baptist, Iviron

Virgin and Child and proceeding to the rest. I have seen this done at the other monasteries also. This practice is to be understood in the light of the Eastern Orthodox teaching regarding icons. The gist of this teaching is given by the following statement of Nikephoros Theotokis(1736-1805), Archbishop of Astrakhan and Stavropol, and one of the most eminent modern Greek theologians: «The Orthodox do not deify, nor worship the holy icons, but through them lift up the mind to the persons represented, venerating and kissing them out of their aspiration and love for the prototypes»(*Kyriakodromion — Book of the Sunday Gospel Passages,* Moscow, 1796, Vol. 2, p. 533).

At the end of the liturgy the priest comes out of the sanctuary, stands in front of the Beautiful Gate and gives blessed bread *(antidoron)* to the monks and laymen who have attended the service. As he hands it to each one, he says: «May the blessing and grace of the Lord come upon you.»

The chanting at Iviron was very good. The articulation both of the right and the left chanters was distinct, the tempo was neither unduly fast nor too slow, and the voices were beautiful. A few compositions, such as the Cherubic Hymn, were sung slowly, as they are meant to be sung. No concession has been made at this or the other Greek monasteries on Athos to Western music. The ancient Christian tradition of antiphonal, monophonic, purely vocal music, which was transmitted by the Byzantines, has been preserved.

In speaking about the time system employed on the Mountain, I mentioned the fact the the Monastery of Iviron is unique in using the Chaldean system, taking sunrise for twelve o'clock. There is another respect, one of major import, in which Iviron is unique among the monasteries of Athos: its involvement in missionary work. This has been excellently summed up by Archimandrite Gabriel of Dionysiou, in his book *Lausaïkon of the Holy Mountain* (p. 61). For centuries, writes Gabriel, the Monastery of Iviron has spread its spiritual fragrance to Orthodox countries as far as the Caucasus and Russia. «From this monastery have been sent as missionaries to those remote countries Fathers virtuous and venerable, Fathers full of love and self-denial, Fathers who were faithful keepers of the injunctions of Paul, according to which there is neither Greek nor barbarian, but Christ is all and in all» (Col. 3: 11). «Iviron,» adds Gabriel, «is the only monastery of Athos that has been sympathetic to the missionary spirit in monasticism. This spirit it still retains. One will find monks from Iviron in America, South Africa, Australia, and elsewhere. These monks serve the spiritual needs of Orthodox and spread their light among all.»

MONASTERY OF VATOPEDI

From Iviron I went by sea to the Monastery of Vatopedi, which lies northwestward on the same side of the peninsula, near the shore. The motorboat that connects the monasteries on this side of the peninsula with one another

VATOPEDI

and with Ierissos arrived at Vatopedi in an hour, after stopping at the monasteries of Stavronikita and Pantocratoros. Vatopedi is the wealthiest monastery on Athos and one of the oldest, having been founded between 972 and 980. It is also one of the most official and largest. From a distance it looks like a mediaeval city.

When I entered the gate, the porter looked at my letter of admission and then led me up a stairway to the guest quarters. Here I was promptly given a room and was served lunch in a small dining room. I ate alone, as the other guests had already eaten. Some time after lunch, I was invited to the spacious and majestic *synodikon,* the room where the senior monks who govern the monastery, the *epitropoi* and the *proistamenoi,* hold their meetings and formally receive official guests. I was received here by the *epitropoi* rather ceremoniously; and after the assistant guestmaster had served us coffee, I was asked various questions regarding America, philosophy, and other subjects. There was something affected in the way these monks spoke, but nonetheless what they said impressed me as being in general sound. Most of the talking was done by Hilarion, the physician of the monastery — a stocky middle-aged monk with small blue eyes and many gold-crowned teeth. He had good things to say about the United States.

«People in America,» remarked Hilarion, «are industrious and upright. You know, there is connection between industriousness and uprightness on the one hand, and laziness and crookedness on the other. The Greek word *radiourgos* is derived from the ancient word *radios,* which means lazy. A *radiourgos* is a lazy person who seeks to acquire goods not by means of work but through intrigue, through cunning.»

Our talk lasted about half an hour. Then I was taken to the library, which I had expressed a desire to see. The library occupies three rooms of moderate size, one above the other, in the tower of defense. It comprises about eleven thousand printed books and over sixteen hundred manuscripts, all of them kept in glass-doored bookcases. This library is one of the very best on the Holy Mountain.

The librarian removed a number of very old, beautiful manuscripts from the shelves and displayed them. He also showed me the *Iaspis,* a jasper cup with a gold base and gold handles — a gift of the Byzantine Emperor Manuel Comnenos Palaiologos (1391-1425), and a remarkable Byzantine fresco, a remnant of a fourteenth century composition, with the heads of the Apostles Peter and Paul.

After my visit to the library, I returned to my room. As I looked at it carefully, I felt an incongruity between it and the very austere spirit that prevails elsewhere on Mount Athos. Here were a sumptuous bed and draperies, a large mirror — the only mirror I had seen thus far on the Mountain — beautiful linoleum on the floor, a fancy electric lamp. The lamp, however, was useless, as the monastery's generator was unserviceable. Lighting was supplied by kerosene lamps. Across from this room was one similar to it. This was occupied by the bishop of Edessa, Macedonia, who was visiting Vatopedi and other monasteries on the Mountain. These two rooms are on either side of the guest hall, which is a large salon with beautiful lounges, armchairs, and rugs. Vatopedi is unique among the monasteries of Athos in having deviated from the traditional Athonite simplicity and austerity, as well as in having abandoned the Julian calendar and the Byzantine time system.

Supper was served in a large dining room of the guesthouse. This time I ate with eleven other guests, including the bishop, two Belgian college students, and two Germans. After supper, we all gathered in the guest hall and talked for an hour or so before retiring.

Early in the morning I was awakened by the rhythmic sounds of the large church bells, which were soon followed by those of the *semantron,* summoning the monks and the more pious guests to church. The large bells are rung only on Sundays and major festivals, or when a bishop or other dignitary is visiting a monastery.

Vatopedi's *katholikon* was built in the tenth or eleventh

century, and is dedicated to the Annunciation of the Theotokos. It is one of the largest churches on the Mountain and is unique in its possession of wall mosaics. These consist of the Annunciation, comprising the figures of the Theotokos and the Archangel Gabriel on either side of the central door that leads from the outer to the inner narthex; a Deësis above the same door, depicting Christ at the center, seated on a throne and flanked on either side by the Virgin and St. John the Baptist; a representation of the Annunciation in the nave, consisting of the Archangel Gabriel on the area above the column that supports the northeast part of the dome and the Theotokos on the corresponding area over the southeast column. The Deësis was probably made at the close of the eleventh century, while the others seem to be works of a somewhat later date. Besides these, there are two miniature mosaics in the sanctuary of the church, one of them depicting St. Anna holding the child Theotokos, and the other the Crucifixion of Christ. Of the large mosaics, the Deësis is the best, while both of the miniatures are superb works, showing astonishing patience and skill, and deep piety. I have been told that another mosaic of Vatopedi, dating from the eleventh century and depicting St. John Chrysostom, is now in the possession of Dumbarton Oaks Research Library and Collection, at Washington, D.C.

The *katholikon* is also decorated with many frescoes, which were painted in 1312. These need to be cleaned of the soot that has accumulated on them during the centuries and of later, disfiguring additions, before their beauty and power can become fully manifest. Further, this church contains many excellent panel icons dating from the Byzantine period. A number of these are to be seen in the sanctuary and include seven panels depicting the Apostles, done in the fourteenth century, and a small diptych depicting Christ on the left leaf and the Virgin and Child on the right. This diptych dates from the eighth century, and is known as «the *Ninia.*» According to tradition, it belonged to the Byzantine Empress Theodora, who kept it secretly during the period of iconoclasm.

In the north side chapel, which is dedicated to St. Demetrios, there are some fine frescoes that were painted in 1721 by imitators of Panselinos. Especially noteworthy among these is the Choir of Hierarchs.

On the iconostasis of the Chapel of the Aghia Zoni «the Holy Girdle,» which is on the slope of the immense stone-paved courtyard, there are three important panels. One of them depicts Christ, the other St. John the Theologian, and the third St. John the Forerunner (or Baptist). The last is the finest and best preserved of the three. The prophet is depicted in an olive-green garment, with uncut, curly hair and beard, quiet, meditative face, and hands raised in prayer and pointing to Christ, Whose icon is to his right. The whole figure is full of dignity and holiness.

Among the other things that caught my attention as I walked about were the figures of Plato, Aristotle, and some other ancients, painted in the vestibule at the gate that leads into the courtyard. I stopped and examined them carefully. These two famous philosophers of Antiquity, together with the «Wise Apollo,» the «Wise Sibylla,» the «Wise Sophocles,» and another ancient, whose name I could not make out, are painted without haloes. Plato holds a scroll on which the following is written: «The old is new and the new is ancient. The father is in the offspring and the offspring is in the father, the one is divided into three, and the three constitute one.» Aristotle, too, holds a scroll, on which is written: «The begetting of God is by nature inexhaustible, for the Logos derives His substance from Him.» The statements are not actually to be found in the writings of the two philosophers. These frescoes, which were painted in 1858 by a certain Nikephoros, are mediocre

THE PROPHET MOSES

Fresco, Side Chapel of St. Demetrios, Vatopedi

as works of art; but from a religious point of view they are very interesting, because they show the attitude of Athonite monks — at least of those of Vatopedi in modern times — towards the ancient Greeks, particularly towards Plato and Aristotle. Being painted here, near the entrance of the monastery, holding scrolls with statements akin to those contained in Christian teaching, the figures of these ancients remind one of the attitude of some of the early Christian writers of the East, such as Clement of Alexandria, that Greek philosophy, as represented by such thinkers, is a pathway leading to Christianity. On the area above the philosophers and the other ancients are depicted saints and angels with haloes. In this way, the artist indicated the general view of the Eastern Fathers that Christianity is something higher than ancient Greek culture even at its best.

In the evening of my third day at Vatopedi, after supper, I talked with Father Theophilos, one of the senior monks of the monastery, about the relationship between Christianity and philosophy, and about monasticism. The conversation developed as we were sitting on the balcony of the guest hall, where a cool, refreshing breeze was coming from the sea. During our discussion, Theophilos assigned much value to philosophy in relation to religion.

«One cannot become a great theologian,» he remarked, «without being to some extent a philosopher. However, a philosophical predisposition, which is a gift, is more important for a theologian than philosophical learning. As far as particular philosophical systems are concerned, to my mind, Platonism is the best. I believe that the association of Eastern Orthodoxy with Plato has been far more fortunate than that of the Western Church with Aristotle. Platonism has more vitality than Aristotelianism; it has more in it that is enduring, and is more likely to remain throughout the centuries a living system making Christianity accessible to intellectuals.»

Regarding the fundamental principles governing monasticism, Theophilos said:

«Monasticism is based on three virtues: 1) poverty *(aktimosyni)*, 2) chastity *(parthenia)*, and 3) obedience *(ypakoui)*. The last two are but forms of the first. Poverty is not to desire to possess anything. Chastity is not to desire anything in the way of carnal pleasures. Obedience is to give up one's will, one's egoism, and to do the will of another, of a spiritual superior.»

What impressed me in these definitions was the reference to an inner, psychological factor, rather than to an outer, physical one, and the conception of this inner factor as a limit, an ideal that is exceedingly difficult to attain. Only true saints can be said to have fully lived up to these high spiritual principles. This led me to ask Theophilos to name some of the saints who have lived at Vatopedi. He mentioned Symeon Nemanya, the founder of the Monastery of Hilandari, who had lived here as a monk for three or four years; Symeon's son Savvas, the greatest Serbian saint; and Maximos the Greek, who exerted an important influence on Russian theology in the sixteenth century and died in Russia in 1556. Maximos translated the Psalter and other liturgic works, and passages from the writings of Eastern Fathers such as St. Isaac the Syrian, St. John Damascene, and St. Symeon the New Theologian. The Russians — though not the Greeks — regard Maximos as a saint.

In answer to my question regarding the daily schedule at Vatopedi, Theophilos told me the following:

«We rise at four o'clock, Western time, and go to church for the *orthros* and the liturgy that immediately follows it. When the liturgy is over, we have coffee. Then, from seven to ten each one of us performs his special tasks *(diakonimata)*, either within the monastery or outside. From ten till twelve we occupy ourselves with various matters at our living quarters, talk with guests, or study. Between twelve and three we have lunch, followed by rest. From three to four we have vespers and the *apodeipnon*. Between four and six we perform our special tasks, and may take a walk when we are not busy. Between six and nine we prepare our evening meal, eat, and study. At nine, we pray in private for about an hour, and then go to bed.

«This schedule,» he went on to explain, «holds during periods when night and day are of about equal duration, but is somewhat different during the other seasons of the year, and considerably different on Sundays, major holy days, days when there are all-night services, and during the long fasting periods.»

BULGARIAN MONASTERY OF ZOGRAPHOU

Zographou, the Bulgarian monastery, is an hour and a half's walk from Vatopedi. It is located inland, closer to the southwestern coast of the peninsula than to the north-

MONASTERY OF ZOGRAPHOU

eastern, and remains invisible until one has come near it, because it is built on a slope close to a valley and is surrounded on all sides by tall vegetation.

This monastery is much smaller than Vatopedi and

has fewer monks: Vatopedi has forty-five, Zographou about thirty-five. By birth, the monks of Zographou are Bulgarians. However, like all the monks on the Mountain, they are Greek subjects, for according to the 1924 Constitutional Charter of Mount Athos, «All those who live the monastic life here [on Athos] become Greek subjects as soon as they are accepted as novices or monks, without any other formality.» Among themselves they speak Bulgarian, but every one of them seems to be able to speak Greek to some extent.

The main church was built in 1801 and was frescoed in 1817. Architecturally it is similar to the *katholika* of the Greek monasteries. Its paintings, however, show certain peculiarities. For instance, the haloes of the large figures that form the lower row of paintings are bas reliefs. Many of the icons have Slavonic inscriptions.

In the nave there is a large icon depicting St. George, to whom the church is dedicated. This icon is said to be *acheiropoietos,* «not made with hands,» but painted miraculously in 980, when the church was first built. It is covered with a sheet of silver, except for the face, which is well executed and full of religious expression.

The church services at Zographou are in Slavonic, but the music is Byzantine. Sometimes it is exactly like that which is heard in the Greek monasteries, at other times it is a slight variation of it.

The rule is coenobitic, and guests may eat in the refectory together with the monks. I shared the simple meals of the monks, and thus had the opportunity of becoming more familiar with the refectory practices at the coenobitic monasteries. I took note of the following. No one touches any food or drink, until the abbot has given permission by striking a bell. When he strikes the bell, eating commences and the reader begins to read. On Sundays and holy days the reader goes up to the pulpit *(ambon)*, while on other days he stands on the floor and sets his book on a book-stand *(analogion)*. When it is time for the meal to stop, the abbot sounds the bell again, and the reader at once stops reading. At this point, a prayer is said and a ceremony is performed, which takes a few minutes. After this, three monks: the reader, the cook, and the monk in charge of the refectory *(trapezaris)*, prostrate themselves at the door and ask the abbot to forgive them for any deficiencies. The last practice is obviously a lesson in humility, both for the three monks who ask for forgiveness and for those who take note of this practice.

Zographou's library has about six thousand books, including over four hundred manuscripts, arranged neatly in glass-doored cases. Most of the printed books and manuscripts are in Slavonic, but there are many Greek works, too, and a smaller number of books in other languages. Among the printed books, I noticed a Slavonic version of the *Philokalia*, named *Dobrotolubiye*.

MONASTERY OF CONSTAMONITOU

Before leaving Zographou, I asked the monks to tell me how to reach the Monastery of Constamonitou, which lies southeast of it. They explained that there is a short cut from Zographou to Constamonitou, but warned me that I would probably get lost if I took that path, and advised me to take instead the broad, not too steep, stone-paved road down to the *arsanas* of their monastery, then to walk along the coast to the *arsanas* of Constamonitou and take the uphill path from there. I followed their advice.

In and about the buildings of the *arsanas* of Zographou I found a dozen or so workmen, some of them eating, others resting and talking. At the pier there were two big motorboats, and several men were busy loading them with timber. A number of youngsters, sons of the workmen, were swimming in the calm, crystal clear sea.

Constamonitou is a small coenobitic monastery, having at present twenty-eight monks. Like Zographou, it is surrounded by mountains, but it has much more of an open view, because on some sides the mountains are distant. Quite near it there is a large vegetable and fruit tree garden that adds to the beauty of the environs. Although Constamonitou was established in the eleventh century, its buildings are not old, as it has been destroyed by fire three times. The main church, similar in form to the older Athonite *katholika,* was built between 1860 and 1871.

The library is in the tower. It is small but well kept and has, besides printed books, more than a hundred manuscripts, among which is a very valuable, eleventh century copy of the *Ladder* of St. John Climacos.

The librarian, Father Modestos, is young, apparently in his early forties, dynamic, and has an excellent memory and deep religious convictions. He regards Eastern Orthodoxy as the highest form of Christianity and Mount Athos as the great center of Orthodox spirituality.

MONASTERY OF CONSTAMONITOU

Inquiring whether the great Byzantine contemplatives are studied here at the present time, I learned that Modestos himself reads, among other ascetic and mystical writings of the Eastern Church, the works of St. Symeon the New Theologian (949-1022), the greatest Byzantine mystic, and the *Philokalia*.

The subject of philosophy came up, and Modestos expressed his attitude towards this subject by quoting the following passage from a manuscript written by an Athonite monk of the post-Byzantine period:

«Many of the Greeks tried to philosophize, but only the monks found and learned the true philosophy. Having received the heavenly gifts in purity and chastity, in fasting, vigilance and prayer, they philosophized saying: ‹The aim of philosophy is to keep the bond of divine love and peace unshaken, to the benefit both of monks and of laymen.›»

Modestos shares this view, which has been expressed by many of the Eastern Fathers, particularly the great mystics.

What writings does Modestos particularly recommend for those who, while living in «the world,» aspire to live as far as possible up to the Christian ideal? In the first place, the Gospels and the rest of the Scriptures. Next, the works of Nicodemos the Aghiorite, especially these: *The Unseen Warfare (O Aoratos Polemos), Handbook of Counsel (Symvouleftikon Encheiridion), Spiritual Exercises (Pnevmatika Gymnasmata), Morality (Chrestoetheia), Garden of Graces (Kipos Hariton),* and the *Philokalia.* He also recommends *Evergetinos,* which, in his words, «teaches a person how to oppose and overcome his inner defects.» Like Maximos of Koutloumousiou, Modestos regards this work as excellent preparatory reading for the *Philokalia.* He holds that one *can* do what these books teach, even if one lives in «the world.»

«But it is necessary,» he explained, «that one have an experienced and competent spiritual guide *(pnevmatikon patera),* whose instructions one follows faithfully, submitting one's will to his. A spiritual guide is indispensable. If a person doesn't have such a guide, he should search for one.»

«Suppose a person makes a search in the city or land where he lives and fails to find a spiritual guide? I asked.

«In such a case, replied Modestos, «he should *correspond* with one on Mount Athos.»

Modestos' assertion that one can do what these books teach even if one lives in the world reminded me of the following statements of St. Symeon the New Theologian that I had read in the *Philokalia:* «Even those who live in the midst of the cares and confusion of ordinary life gain salvation and are accounted worthy of great blessings, provided they order their lives as they ought.... He who wants and longs with all his soul and heart to do what is good and virtuous, receives from the all-powerful God the power to do it no matter where he is....» (2, 511, 512). Modestos' emphasis on the need for a spiritual guide or teacher likewise brought to my mind pertinent statements by St. Symeon and other Greek Fathers. This saint remarks that «without a spiritual father and guide and teacher it is impossible for a man to keep the commandments of God and to live virtuously, and not to be caught by the snares of the Devil» (*Symeon tou Neou Theologou Ta Evriskomena — The Existing Works of St. Symeon the New Theologian,* ed. by D. Zagoraios, Syros, 1886, p. 75). And Nikephoros the Solitary says: «It is necessary to seek a good guide... who will make things clear to us and indicate the mental path without uncertainty, so that we may proceed easily. If there is no such guide in view, we must exert ourselves patiently to find one» (*Philokalia,* 2, 241).

What should a spiritual guide be like? Callistos and Ignatios Xanthopoulos give this description: He should be «free from beguilement—this may be proved by comparing his words with the testimony of the Scriptures — having the Spirit within him, leading a mode of life in conformity with his words, lofty minded yet humble, and in other ways a good man, as a teacher of Christ should be» (*Philokalia,* 2, 353).

MONASTERY OF DOCHEIARIOU

To reach Docheiariou, which is the nearest monastery to the south of Constamonitou, built on a slope near the sea, I had to walk back to the *arsanas* of Constamonitou and then take a path southward along the coast.

Docheiariou is idiorrhythmic. It has about twenty monks, all of them very kindly and hospitable.

As at the other monasteries that I visited, I spent some time exploring the library, which is housed in a room high up in the tall tower that dominates the whole monastery. The catalogue that lists the books is very unsystematic, but the collection itself is by no means negligible: it comprises several thousand printed books and about four hundred manuscripts, some of which were written as far back as the eleventh century.

During the church services, I happened to take special note of the music. The chanting was brisk. The only hymn that was sung slowly, very slowly indeed, was the Cherubic. Both the right and the left chanters stood in the stalls at the eastern end of the semi-circles known as *choroi*, choirs, which are formed by the arms of the transept, and faced westward. I had seen the chanters occupy this part of the choir at the other monasteries, but it was here that I happened to reflect on the matter. Seeking an explanation for the position of the chanters, I concluded that it must have been instituted in order to render the chanting more audible and thereby more effective.

The main church or *katholikon* is a very tall and majestic sixteenth century edifice built at the center of the small and rather steep courtyard. It has five tall domes, two small ones at the eastern end, one over each of the side apses of the sanctuary, two larger ones over the esonarthex or *liti,* and a much larger one, which rises high above the others, over the nave. The general ground plan of the building is the same as that of the other Athonite *katholika:* it is a cross with all the ends, except the western, rounded in the interior. The *liti* is unusually large. The frescoes that adorn it and the nave were painted in 1568, and are outstanding works of the Cretan School of iconography. Among the most striking frescoes is one in the *liti* depicting St. Pachomios standing to the right of an angel. Pachomios, who was one of the great masters of the monastic life and who is said to have founded, about 318, the first Christian monastery, is represented looking at the angel with face, hands and posture expressing deep humility and awe. The angel holds an open scroll on which is written: «In this Habit *(Schema)* shall all flesh be saved, O Pachomios.» This icon is in accordance with a tradition that an angel, dressed as monk, appeared to Pachomios and made the statement that I have quoted, pointing at the monastic mantle and cowl.

ST. PACHOMIOS AND ANGEL
Fresco, katholikon of Docheiariou

Why such emphasis is given to the garb of the monk

is explained by the following remark of St. Ephraim the Syrian, which appears in his *Ascetic Works*: «Humble monk, understand the Habit that you wear and notice how much difference there is between it and that of the worldly man;

THE RESURRECTION
Fresco, katholikon of Docheiariou

and direct your mind to what it means — namely, that it signifies the renunciation of worldly ways and things and reminds one of spiritual work» (p. 119).

The effect of participating in a night service in a

church such as the one described is tremendous. The mysterious power of the architecture is enhanced by the darkness, lit by the faint, trembling light of the candles in the chandeliers. The frescoed figures, especially those on the lower parts of the walls which are within the halo of the lights, acquire a strange dynamism and assume a more awe-inspiring aspect. And the sacred chant, which is executed by two choirs, acts on one with great force in this unearthly atmosphere.

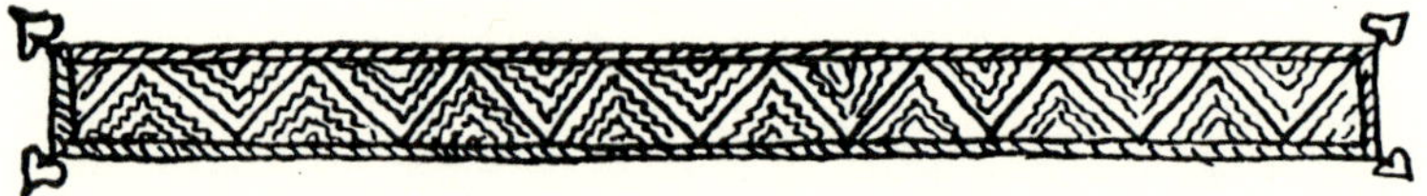

MONASTERY OF XENOPHONTOS

Continuing my journey, I walked to the next monastery southward, Xenophontos, which is only twenty minutes away, near the beach. Xenophontos is larger than Docheiariou, and has at present about thirty monks.

MONASTERY OF XENOPHONTOS

The main church of this monastery is relatively new, having been built between 1809 and 1819, to supersede the old *katholikon,* which was too small for the then expanding monastery. It has very few wall paintings, and these modern and devoid of deep religious expression and artistic merit. Among the panel paintings, there are some that are excellent. The most important icons are two mosaics on panels, said to date from the eleventh or twelfth century. One of them depicts St. Demetrios and the other St. George, nearly life-size, on a gold background. These mosaics are among the few to be seen on the Holy Mountain.

Excellent frescoes, among the best examples of monastic iconography, are to be seen in the Chapel of St. George, the former *katholikon* of the monastery. These paintings were done in 1545 by Anthony the Cretan. Most of them, unfortunately, are marred by the unskilful retouching of a later artist.

ST. DEMETRIOS
Mosaic, katholikon
of Xenophontos

As at some of the other monasteries that I visited, sacred relics, such as part of the True Cross and various bones and bone fragments of saints were exhibited to the guests. These relics are kept in the sanctuary of the *katholikon* in specially made small cases and are regarded with great reverence by the monks. The *bemataris,* or monk who had charge of the sanctuary, explained what each one was, kissed them, and then asked the guests to kiss them too. Some may feel revulsion at the practice of kissing such bones, may regard it as an idolatrous veneration for

ST. EUSTATHIOS
Chapel of St. George, Monastery of Xenophontos

mere matter. But according to Eastern Orthodox teaching, when the soul is sanctified, the body becomes sanctified also. Thus Saint Symeon the New Theologian says:

«The soul that has been accounted worthy of becoming a partaker of Divine Grace, because it has been sanctified, necessarily sanctifies its whole body, since it holds the body together and is present in all its parts. For this reason the Grace of the Holy Spirit, just as it appropriates to itself the soul, so too it appropriates to itself the body. However, as long as the soul is united with the body, the All-Holy Spirit does not bring all of the body fully to its own glory, because it is necessary that the soul show its will until the end of this life. But when the end comes and the soul separates from the body, then, as the struggle has ceased and the soul has won and departs from the body with the wreath of incorruptibility, then, I say, the Grace of the Holy Spirit appropriates to itself and sanctifies fully the body of such a soul. And for this reason the bare bones and the bodies of Saints emit remedies and cure diseases» *(The Existing Works of St. Symeon the New Theologian,* p. 46*)*.

The library is on the ground floor of one of the buildings. It consists of a single medium-sized room containing a good collection of books, including about two hundred manuscripts. Among the printed books I noticed a copy of Dionysios Zagoraios' edition of the works of St. Symeon the New Theologian. As I was examining this book, Archimandrite Evdokimos, the abbot, who took me to the library, remarked:

ST. SYMEON THE NEW THEOLOGIAN

«St. Symeon was a great saint and contemplative, and a theologian that was taught by God *(theodidaktos)*. What he wrote was not the fruit of scholarly learning—he was an unlearned man—but came from Above. For he had purified himself of every vice and had risen to great heights of virtue, and had thus rendered himself a fit vehicle of the Spirit.»

Evdokimos is a man of deep piety. Although he is somewhat reserved, I was able to talk with him for a considerable period of time and to learn his viewpoint on various matters. He manifested an interesting combination of traditional Hellenic sagacity and Christian understanding.

RUSSIAN MONASTERY OF PANTELEIMONOS

The next monastery which I visited on my way south-eastward was that of Panteleïmonos, or the Roussiko, as it is popularly known. It took me an hour of uninterrupted walking on a narrow but for the most part level path to

DOMES OF PANTELEIMONOS

arrive here. The Roussiko is built on a slope near the sea. It is one of the largest monasteries on Athos, comprising very big modern buildings that are four, five, and even six stories high. The showy, green church domes, which are surmounted by onion-shaped gold balls and ornate crosses, distinguish Panteleïmonos sharply from the Greek monasteries.

The history of this monastery is confused, but the essential facts seem to be as follows: In the eleventh or

PANTELEIMONOS

twelfth century, a group of Russian monks moved into the Monastery of Xylourgou, which had been founded by Greeks, probably in the tenth century. The presence of the

Russians in this monastery led to its becoming known as the monastery of the Russians. From here, they moved to another monastery, named Tou Thessalonikeos. Finally, the Russians came to the present monastery of Panteleïmonos, which seems to have been built early in the eighteenth century. During the nineteenth century, the monastery underwent great expansion, as the Russian monks increased until they predominated over the Greeks. The first Russian abbot was elected in 1875.

At present, Panteleïmonos has about eighty-five monks, five of whom are Greeks and the rest Russians. As at the Skete of St. Andrew, most of the monks are very old, in their eighties or nineties. The absence of younger monks is due to the fact that the Holy Community and the Greek government do not admit Russians to Athos as monks, because they fear that this would result in communist infiltration. The last Russians to come to the Roussiko to become monks arrived in 1928.

Church services are performed simultaneously in Slavonic and in Greek, in two different chapels.

The main church is dedicated to St. Panteleïmon. Its icons, both murals and panels, date from the nineteenth and twentieth centuries, and are inspired by Italian Renaissance models. The same type of icons are to be seen in a large chapel that is dedicated to the Holy Veil and St. Alexander Nevsky. This chapel consists of two parallel basilicas separated by a colonnade. It has a tall, dazzlingly bright iconostasis, made of wood that has been plastered and gilded.

The most remarkable feature of the *katholikon* is its bell tower. This has a large number of bells, including one that is the biggest on the Holy Mountain, weighing, I was told, about ten tons.

Panteleïmonos' refectory, too, which was built in 1892, is on a grand scale. It has seats for eight hundred monks.

At that time, such a large refectory was certainly needed; in fact, it was not sufficienty large to accomodate all the monks at one sitting.

My guide at the Roussiko was a middle-aged Greek monk named Photios. Photios has lived in Russia, and knows both Russian and Greek well. He has read widely, not only Orthodox writings, but also religious works of the Far East. Referring to modern religious teachers of the Far East, he singled out Sri Ramakrishna and recommended the *Sayings* of this Hindu.

«Ramakrishna,» he remarked, «followed the Path of Love *(Agapi)*, and was in a way a Christian.»

«Does the library here have this work and the other Far Eastern writings that you have studied?» I asked Photios.

«No,» he replied. «I read these works many years ago, before I came here.»

In connection with the Eastern Orthodox Fathers, I asked Photios which of them he especially studied.

«St. Symeon the New Theologian is one of my favorite Fathers,» he replied. «St. Symeon writes about important things with great clarity and contrition. St. Macarios the Great, St. Isaac the Syrian, and St. Gregory the Theologian are among my other favorite Church Teachers. I find St. Gregory extremely luminous.»

MONASTERY OF LAVRA

From the Roussiko I went by motorboat to the nearby port of Daphne, and from there to the Monastery of Lavra, which is far away, on the southeastern corner of the peninsula. The boat left Daphne around noon and arrived in the small but very picturesque harbor of Lavra at 3:30, after stopping at the landing places of several monasteries and sketes and letting off or picking up passengers, and giving out mail and food supplies.

HARBOR OF LAVRA

Lavra is built on a plateau about twenty minutes from the harbor, and is reached by a steep, twisting, stone-paved path. It was founded in 963, and is the oldest Athonite monastery, and one of the largest and most official. Despite the sharp decline in the number of monks in the monasteries of the Holy Mountain since the Second World War, there are today in this monastery about eighty monks and three novices. Its system is idiorrhythmic.

On the day of my arrival I met one of the most noteworthy monks of Lavra, Father Avvakum. He was barefooted and wore ragged clothes. From my talk with him I learned that he used to be a hermit, living in a hut about an hour's walk from Lavra, but had been urged to return to the monastery because it was in need of hands. He considered his coming back a great sacrifice, because for him as for the Fathers of the Eastern Church

MONASTERY OF LAVRA

the life of a hermit represents a more advanced stage of spiritual development than life in a monastery, providing, for those who are well prepared for it, more favorable conditions for inner concentration and higher religious experience. But he had the consolation that he was allowed to return to his hermitage at intervals, whenever he felt a great need for absolute solitude.

One of the subjects we touched upon was iconography. A lay artist who took part in our conversation praised the works of an iconographer named Ioannikios Mavropoulos, who has done some icons for Lavra, while Avvakum criticized Ioannikios' works, saying that the figures depicted in them expressed carnal instead of spiritual beauty. He attributed this to Ioannikios' lack of true religious inspiration. Avvakum's standpoint was that of the Byzantine art tradition, according to which the painting of true icons is a sacred activity that requires not merely skill, but also deep piety and Divine Grace, and seeks to express spirit-

KATHOLIKON OF LAVRA AND SIDE CHAPEL
South side

ual rather than physical beauty. Father Avvakum took us into the *katholikon* and the refectory, and indicated some of the distinctive features of Byzantine iconography.

The frescoes in the main part of the *katholikon* and those of the refectory are works of the leader of the Cretan School of iconography on the Mountain, Theophanes the Cretan, a monk, and of his two sons, who likewise were monks. This church is the oldest one on Athos. It was

ST. MACARIOS, PATRIARCH OF JERUSALEM
Detail from the Elevation of the Holy Cross
Fresco, katholikon of Lavra

built in 963 by St. Athanasios the Athonite, founder of the monastery, with the financial assistance of his close friend, the Byzantine Emperor Nikephoros Phocas, who also assisted him in the construction of the rest of the monastery. The frescoes were painted in 1535. In spite of their age, the church and its murals and those of the refectory are well preserved. They are great works of art.

Besides the wall paintings of Theophanes and his sons, many of the panel icons in the *katholikon* are superb examples of Byzantine art. I might mention a group of small icons that hang upon the walls of the south choir and depict the Transfiguration, the Entrance into Jerusalem, the Crucifixion, the Removal from the Cross, the Ascension, and other New Testament events. These icons, as one of the younger and better educated monks, Elias, explained to me, constituted the upper tier of small icons of the older iconostasis. (In a Greek Orthodox church, two rows of icons are placed on the iconostasis, a lower row of large icons and an upper row of small ones. The lower row includes the following: immediately to the north of the Beautiful Gate, the icon of Christ, and next to it, that of St. John the Baptist; and immediately to the south of the Beautiful Gate, the icon of the Holy Virgin and Child, and next to it that of the sacred person or persons, or event, to which the church is dedicated. The row of small icons, on the upper part of the iconostasis, comprises representations of the following twelve major events from the life of Christ: the Annunciation, the Nativity, the Presentation of Christ in the Temple, the Baptism, the Transfiguration, the Raising of Lazarus, the Entrance into Jerusalem, the Crucifixion, the Resurrection, the Ascension, the Pentecost, and the Dormition of the Virgin. Sometimes the icons of the Twelve Apostles are used instead.) These beautiful panels are no longer on the iconostasis, because some innovators of the last century, impressed by the very high and complex

THE ELEVATION OF THE HOLY CROSS
Detail, fresco, katholikon of Lavra

iconostases that had been introduced by the Russian monks of Athos into their own churches, took apart the older iconostasis in 1870, replaced it with one of Russian design, and mounted modern icons upon it like those made by the Russians. The new iconostasis is a major incongruity in the church, spoiling its interior. Instead of the traditional single tier of small icons above the first tier of large ones, it has five tiers. Being too high, it conceals entirely the wonderful Holy Virgin in the apse of the sanctuary, as well as other fine frescoes in that part of the church — the Ascension, the Last Supper, the Hierarchs, etc. And its icons, with the exception of two, being modern, secularized, devoid of deep religious feeling, are totally unrelated to the splendid Byzantine frescoes and panels. The two icons I have excepted are those of Christ and of the Holy Virgin. These were probably retained from the older iconostasis.

While in the *katholikon* studying the frescoes and panel icons, I noticed certain round perforations in the pendentives of the main dome. There are three openings in the southeast pendentive, two in the northeast pendentive, and one in each of the other two pendentives. I have seen similar perforations in other Byzantine churches. Fotis Kontoglous, the eminent Greek iconographer and restorer, who has had occasion to work in the domes of many Byzantine churches and to examine them closely, once told me that these holes are the mouths of clay pitchers which the Byzantines put in the pendentives when they were building the churches, for the purpose of enhancing the sonority of the chanting.

The refectory, which faces the *katholikon,* has the shape of a cross and is one of the finest, best preserved, and largest on the Mountain, having twenty-four marble tables, each for fourteen to eighteen monks. All its walls are covered with frescoes, both compositions and representations of individual saints. Among the most remarkable compositions is one that depicts All the Saints Entering Paradise. This painting is near the entrance of the refectory, on the right side as one enters. Depicted here is a procession of tall, slim, upright figures full of piety, with gestures of prayer and heads surrounded with prominent haloes. At the front of the procession one can distinguish the Apostles Peter, Paul, and John. Some of the frescoes have been retouched by later painters, and certain of them seem to be in their entirety works of a later date.

Many excellent panel icons are to be seen in the little Chapel of St. Michael Synadon. This chapel has actually been made a museum of Byzantine iconography. Numerous old icons of all sizes and depicting a great variety of themes have been hung all over the walls.

Besides its remarkable main church, refectory, and

REFECTORY OF LAVRA

chapel-museum, the Monastery of Lavra can boast of the most beautiful phiale or sacred fountain on the Holy Mountain. This phiale, which stands in front of the *katholikon,* about a yard west of the entrance, and dates from the eleventh century, consists of a basin with a dome above it that rests on eight columns connected at the upper end by round brick arches and at the lower part by sculptured marble slabs. The basin is carved out of a single block of white marble and is about eight feet in diameter. The phiale is used for preparing holy water *(aghiasmos)* on the first day of each month, with the exception of January, when it is used on Theophany day.

The library and treasure room of Lavra are in an isolated, one-storied, three-room stone building located behind the main church. In the room at the north end of the building are kept the printed books, which constitute a very important collection. In the middle room are kept the manuscripts—2,200 of them, making up the largest and best manuscript collection on the Mountain. Some of the manuscripts contain remarkable miniature icons, among the finest I have ever seen. The dates of the manuscripts vary widely; some of them go as far back as the fourth century A.D. At the south end of the building is the treasure room, which contains the largest and most valuable collection of precious articles on Athos. Among the things kept here are a *sakkos* (a robe worn on very solemn occasions)—said to have belonged to Nikephoros Phocas—richly wrought with gold, an emperial crown, mitres of archbishops, gold and silver staffs, beautiful vestments of bishops and priests, crosses, two huge Books of the Gospels—one Greek, weighing 39 pounds and the other Russian, weighing 62 pounds—adorned with a large quantity of gold, and some superb panel icons.

One evening, as I was strolling in the courtyard, I came upon Avvakum, sitting on the ground a short distance from the main church, holding a small cubical lantern and talking with another monk, who was standing. Avvakum recognized me and asked me to join them. The limited area that was illuminated by the lantern caused my vision to be focussed on Avvakum. I took special note of his thin, ascetic face and his hardy hands. On his knuckles I noticed conspicuous calluses, the result of the many prostrations that he performed daily. As to how many prostrations or kneelings should be performed by those who have chosen the contemplative and monastic life, I shall quote the following succint statement of Callistos and Ignatios Xanthopoulos: «Concerning the number of kneelings, we know that our holy Fathers have prescribed three hundred, which we must perform every day and night of the five weekdays. For we have been commanded to rest from them on Saturdays and Sundays and also on other days and weeks that have been noted as exceptions through custom for certain mystical and secret reasons. Some persons, however, perform more than this number, others less, each according to his strength and deliberate choice. Therefore, you, too, do according to your strength. Yet blessed indeed is he who in this as in other godly acts does more, forcing himself; for the kingdom of heaven suffereth violence, and the violent take it by force» (*Philokalia,* 2, 375). The practice of prostrating oneself has two aspects, one outer and the other inner. It serves both to exercise the body, and to call forth painful voluntary efforts and to evoke contrition. Regarding the latter, Theoleptos, a contemporary of Callistos and Ignatios who at first led a life of spiritual struggle on Mount Athos and then became Metropolitan of Philadelphia in Asia Minor, says this: «You should not neglect kneeling. For kneeling represents falling into sin and also a confession of sin. Rising up signifies repentance and a promise to lead a virtuous life. Let every kneeling be made with a mental invocation of Jesus, so that by falling with both soul and body at the feet of the Lord, you may win the benevolence of the God of souls and bodies» (*Philokalia,* 2, 231).

To return to Avvakum, when I joined him and the other monk, he started reciting passages from Scripture. Now and then he would stop his recitation and ask me:

«What does that mean?»

If I replied that I did not know, Avvakum would say: «Listen, then.»

And he would start interpreting it. The first thing he quoted was St. Paul's statement that «The love of money

MONASTERY OF LAVRA

THE HOLY VIRGIN AND CHILD

Panel icon on the iconostasis
of the katholikon, Lavra

CHRIST

Panel icon on the iconostasis
of the katholikon, Lavra

is the root of all evil» (1 Tim. 6: 10). This apparently was intended as a warning to me against what he, like many other persons in Greece, regards as the typical weakness of Americans. At one point I asked him:

«Father Avvakum, what is your attitude towards philosophy?»

«True philosophy, my son,» he replied, «is to be found in the Gospels, in the Epistles of the Apostle Paul and elsewhere in the Scriptures, and also in the writings of the Fathers and in the lives of saints. What is generally called philosophy is, in comparison with these, worthless. Listen to what Paul says in his First Epistle to Timothy: ‹Avoid the godless chatter and contradictions of what is falsely called knowledge, for by professing it some have missed the mark as regards the faith.›»

Although unlettered, Avvakum possesses an astonishing knowledge of the Scriptures. He can recite from memory, rapidly and accurately, page after page of the Old and New Testaments, and give illuminating interpretations.

«How have you acquired this ability?» I asked Avvakum.

«It is a result of daily study and of chastity, and above all a gift of the Divine Spirit,» he replied.

What does chastity have to do with the matter? one might ask. According to the Eastern Fathers, chastity is one of the necessary conditions for becoming a recipient of the Divine Spirit. Thus, St. Ephraim the Syrian, a favorite author on Mount Athos, says: «Acquire chastity that the Holy Spirit may come to dwell in thee» (*Ascetic Works*, p. 120).

The picture of Avvakum as I saw him that evening will forever remain vividly in my mind: a barefooted, bright-eyed, benign old monk sitting on the ground in the quiet, dark courtyard, holding his little lantern with his left hand, quoting and interpreting passages from the Holy Scriptures.

KERASIA AND KATOUNAKIA

In the evening of my third day at Lavra it started raining. The rain continued through the night and morning. It was the first rain on the Holy Mountain in five months — since May. At the same time, a strong wind was blowing and the sea was rough, and hence it was impossible for a motorboat to come to the harbor of Lavra in the morning and take the guests who wanted to leave.

I set out by foot for Kerasia, a dependency of Lavra, situated to its southwest, high up on the Mountain, about two and a half thousand feet above the sea. I arrived in Kerasia at noon, four hours after my departure. The road was uphill nearly all of the way, and sometimes it was very steep. Yet I walked very briskly and without stopping to rest, because after the first hour it rained or drizzled continuously, my clothes got wet, and I wanted to reach my destination as soon as possible in order to dry myself. During the journey, my field of vision was obscured by the mist and clouds through which I walked.

When I was near Kerasia, I saw a little house and proceeded to it, with the hope that the hermits there would have a fire, where I could dry my clothes. In the house I found two kindly Rumanian monks, but no fire nor even firewood. The hermits offered me some grapes and walnuts which they had gathered from their garden, and instructed me where to go for better hospitality.

Resuming my journey, I soon arrived at a house, used

by lay workers, with a big fire burning at the hearth. I was now in Kerasia, which consists of about ten houses, most of them small and inhabited by two or three monks each.

When I had dried myself, one of the workmen directed me to the nearby Russian Kelli of St. George, which provides hospitality to visitors. This *kelli* has the largest building in Kerasia. Although only three monks dwell in it now, it had at one time as many as thirty.

Late in the afternoon, having recuperated, I left this house and proceeded further southwest to Katounakia, which is another dependency of the Monastery of Lavra, consisting of a group of thirty or so *kalyves,* most of them very small, widely interspersed over a rocky area and inhabited by some fifty monks. The rain had now stopped, the sun had come out, and everything looked fresh and transfigured. I reached Katounakia after an hour and a half of downhill walking, and went to the house of the Danielaioi, which is inhabited by nine monks, four of whom are young while the others are middle aged or old. The building of this brotherhood is a modern, long, three-storied, thirteen-room structure that stands in sharp contrast to the other dwellings of this area, which are very humble, small, one-storied huts or caves. However, it is the only house in this region where visitors who want to stay overnight can find accomodations. And the hospitality offered here is truly excellent.

Five of the monks of this house devote themselves chiefly to iconography. Orders for icons are sent to the house from various parts of Greece and also from abroad. The master icon painter of the brotherhood is a genial elderly monk named Gerontios.

My study of the icons done here, and my talks about iconography with Gerontios, made the following clear to me. Up until recently these monks, like most of the other icon painters on Athos, have been following the dominant iconographic trend that started in Greece in the nineteenth century, that of abandoning the Byzantine tradition of painting and employing instead Russian and Italian Renaissance prototypes and techniques. During the last few years, however, these monks and many others on the Mountain

HERMITS

have begun to return to the Byzantine tradition, so that they now paint not only modern but also Byzantine icons. How is this to be explained? I believe that the cleaning of the frescoes and panel icons of the Protaton, which exposed the full sublimity of these works, the interest which Greek archeologists, such as Xyngopoulos, have shown in these paintings, the admiration which visitors from other countries have in recent years been expressing for them, and the spirited defense of Byzantine art by Kontoglous (see my book *Byzantine Sacred Art*), all have contributed to this fortunate new trend, which will probably gain force with the passage of time, as more frescoes and panel icons of Mount Athos are cleaned and as the understanding and appreciation of Byzantine art increase.

With Father Stephen, the eldest member of the brotherhood, I talked about the relations of the founder of the house, the monk Daniel of Smyrna (1844-1929), to the outstanding Greek philosopher and theologian Apostolos Makrakis (1831-1905) and his followers. Daniel was an icon painter, but he is better known as a critic of Makrakis.

«Daniel,» said Father Stephen, the eldest member of the brotherhood, «has played an important part in the critical confrontation of Makrakis' teaching, both orally and through his writings. Archimandrite Philotheos Zervakos, abbot of the Monastery of Longovarda, in Paros, once came here to discuss Makrakis' teaching with Daniel. At the time of his arrival, Philotheos was an ardent follower of Makrakis, and hoped to win Daniel over to Makrakis' teaching. When he left, Philotheos was no longer a Makrakist. Daniel had convinced him that Makrakis had gone astray in a number of important matters. And when he returned to Longovarda, Philotheos gathered all of the writings of Makrakis then in the monastery and committed them to the flames and anathematized Makrakis.»

«This subject interests me considerably,» I remarked. «I have read a number of works both by Makrakis and by Philotheos, and would appreciate it very much if you could give me copies of Daniel's writings. I promise to send them back to you after reading them.»

«Unfortunately, most of Daniel's writings remain unpublished. But I shall give you copies of those that have appeared in print. You can keep these.»

Thereupon Stephen went to the library and brought me two small books by Daniel, one on the Russian Monastery of Panteleïmonos, where he had lived for a time, and one on Makrakis.

What, in brief, are Daniel's criticisms of Makrakis? On reading the booklet on Makrakis, I found the following especially pertinent critical assertions: Makrakis, although at first a great teacher, later became a great heresiarch, teaching 1) that man is not of a dual nature (body and soul), but is tricomposite, made up of body, soul, and spirit; 2) that the soul was created of dust of the earth and returns to the earth, like that of the brutes; 3) that the soul of man is an inert and irrational substance; 4) that the third element in man is the very eternal Spirit of the triune God; and 5) that Christ was imperfect before He was baptized and then became perfect. On all of these points, Makrakis is contradicted by the Holy Scriptures and the writings of the Greek Fathers.

How, asks Daniel, did Makrakis fall into such heresies? He answers: «The chief cause which led Makrakis astray into so many gross innovations is was the high esteem he had for his own wisdom and knowledge, having through sophistical arguments and syllogistic proofs sought to identify human knowledge with divine revelation. Our divinely inspired Fathers, on the other hand, teach us to accept things divine through faith, and not through knowledge, through the power of the Spirit, and not through dialectical validity. «The simplicity of faith,» says St. Basil, «is stronger than logical demonstrations.» And St. Chrysostom says: «God revealed things to us through His Spirit, and not through outer wisdom.»

Daniel does not condemn philosophy and other secular knowledge, but only the substitution of these for revealed knowledge, and the placing of them on the same level as revelation. He says: «It is true that secular knowledge and wisdom are good and useful, and contribute much to the development and moral education of man, in that they find the reasons of things; but they are limited only to the realm of nature and do not possess validity in the realm that is above nature.»

In conclusion, Daniel calls attention to the unanimity of the Church Fathers on the doctrines of the Orthodox Faith and also to their extreme moderation and humility, and contrasts them in these respects with the egotistic tendency of Makrakis, his innovations, his insults to the Fathers, and his praise of himself.

Daniel's critique of Makrakis is one of the most apt and concise that I have come across.

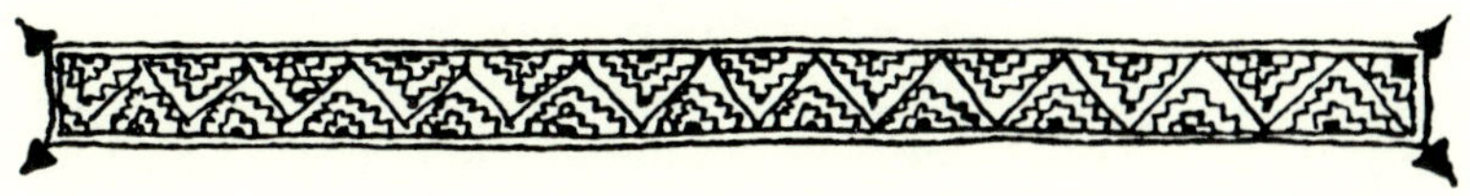

MONASTERY OF ST. PAUL

Leaving Katounakia, I headed by foot for the Monastery of St. Paul, taking a track that passes through the Skete of St. Anne, situated on a very steep terraced slope, a good distance from the sea. During my journey, which

MONASTERY OF ST. PAUL

took about two hours, I paused at this skete in order to rest and drink some cold, refreshing water from a stream that runs through this region, and also to visit the main church.

The Monastery of St. Paul was founded in the tenth

century by St. Paul of Xeropotamou. This saint, according to tradition, was the son of the Byzantine emperor Michael Rangave, and is said to have been invited by the then Kral (ruler) of Serbia, where he became «another Apostle, thoroughly enlightening Serbia with his most

THE LAST SUPPER

wise teachings, leading the nation of the Serbs from unbelief to belief.» Although St. Paul's was founded at that early date, neither its present *katholikon* nor the refectory are old. The *katholikon* was built between 1817 and 1845, and has no murals. The refectory, which is west of it, seems to be more recent and has only three wall paintings. One of them depicts the Mystical («Last») Supper—a reminder that the practice of taking meals in common, which is followed by coenobia, has been taught by Christ's own example.

In one of the old buildings of the quadrangle there is a tiny chapel dedicated to St. George. This chapel is decorated with wonderful frescoes of the Cretan School, dating from 1553. Many of these frescoes are in a poor state of preservation and some have totally perished. Among the most outstanding and best preserved are those depicting St. Pachomios with an angel, Sts. Peter and Paul embracing each other, and St. John the Theologian. The icons of the iconostasis are also of high artistic merit.

There are some fine old panel icons in the Chapel of St. Anthimos, too, and a very expressive remnant of a fresco depicting St. Athanasios the Athonite, founder of the Monastery of Lavra. This painting seems to have survived from the old *katholikon* of St. Paul's.

Among the vicissitudes through which this monastery has passed is a fire that broke out in 1902 and destroyed half of the monastery, including a large part of the library. The edifices have been rebuilt. And the library, in spite of its losses, has today about a hundred manuscripts and a good collection of printed books.

Like the other monasteries on Athos, the number of monks St. Paul's has at present—forty—is rather small for its size. However, the abbot and other leading monks here are hopeful of better days, and are doing some valuable work for attracting more persons to Athonite monasticism. Since 1950, they have been publishing a periodical entitled *St. Paul of Xeropotamou (Aghios Pavlos o Xeropotamitis)*, which presents informative and edifying material regarding monasticism in general and Athonite monasticism in particular. It is distributed free, not only in Greece, but also abroad. Further, to improve the financial condition of their monastery, in order to provide for a larger number of monks, they recently constructed an automobile road that connects their main forests, high up on the mountain, with the *arsanas,* and bought a truck — the first automobile to appear on Athos — to carry the timber down to the landing place. The truck has replaced the many mules and workmen that were formerly employed by the monastery, thus cutting down expenses considerably. The monks of other, more conservative monasteries look upon this innovation very critically as one which, if extensively imitated, will spoil the Byzantine character of the Holy Mountain and will lead to excessive tourism there, destroying the seclusion that they now enjoy.

Among the monks of St. Paul's I had occasion to talk with at length was a seventy-five year old former hermit named Gerasimos Menagias. Gerasimos has been on Mount Athos for thirty-five years, all of which except one he has spent as a hermit, first at St. Basil and later at Little St. Anne. St. Basil is a small settlement of hermits on the southwestern slope of Mount Carmel, far above Katounakia, in an arid area where the terrain is so abrupt that it is very difficult for a person to walk; while Little St. Anne is a short distance from Katounakia. Father Gerasimos found it necessary to abandon the extremely severe life of a hermit when he developed heart trouble. He entered this monastery and has been serving as its pharmacist. I may note here that the health of a number of Athonite monks I have talked with was far from perfect, although as a group the monks of Athos are rather healthy and live to a ripe old age. The Monastery of St. Paul has no physician and no trained pharmacist, but somehow the monks who act as such do satisfactorily. Serious cases are sent to Thessaloniki or Athens.

From my conversation with Gerasimos I learned also

THE APOSTLES PETER AND PAUL
Fresco, Chapel of St. George, Monastery of St. Paul

the following. He studied at the University of Zurich, Switzerland, for six years and received a degree in chemistry. When he left Switzerland, he returned to Greece and worked as a chemist. Later he went to Egypt, where he worked in the same field.

How did he become interested in religion?

«In my early youth,» said Gerasimos, «I was indifferent to religion. In my later student days, however, I began to be impressed by telepathy, clairvoyance, mediumistic and other psychic phenomena, and gradually became convinced of the existence of the soul and of a world of spiritual beings. Exactly what their nature was did not concern me very much. The important thing for me was that such entities did really exist. Later, when still a student, I became so interested in religion, that I would have come to the Holy Mountain at once, had I not been prevented from doing so by my brother and mother.

«While in Switzerland,» he went on, «I fell in love with a German girl. I was intensely in love with her, so that I wanted to see her constantly, and thought of her all the time, even in my dreams. But with the growth of my interest in religion, my love shifted to God. I came to love God much more than I had loved her. And I wanted to live the quiet, contemplative life of a monk, dedicated to the unceasing adoration of Him.»

MONASTERY OF DIONYSIOU

Departing from the Monastery of St. Paul, I walked down to the beautiful pebble-covered beach, which is about fifteen minutes away. When I arrived there, a rowboat was ready to leave for the next monastery northwestward, Dionysiou. The owner of the boat, a layman, welcomed me in. Dionysiou is built near the sea, on top of a massive, high, abrupt rock, and rises to six stories on the south side and four on the others. It can be reached from St. Paul's either by boat or by foot. The path that leads there begins from the beach, continues up a very steep slope, and then levels off. I made the journey by this path in 1952, and covered the distance in about an hour.

The Monastery of Dionysiou was founded in 1355 by St. Dionysios of Korysos, Kastoria, and was enlarged in 1375, with the financial assistance of Alexis, king of Trebizond. It has forty-five monks, five of whom, including the abbot, are priests, one is a deacon, and four are novices. These figures were given to me by Archimandrite Gabriel, who has been abbot of the monastery since 1936, and is one of the most distinguished monks of Athos today.

On the day of my arrival at Dionysiou, there was an all-night vigil service *(agrypnia)*, which started at 7:45 and continued without interruption for eight hours. It was one of the shorter vigil services—there are others that go on for twelve to fifteen hours. Father Theocletos, the secretary and maintainer-of-the-rules *(typikaris)* of the monastery, urged me to attend this service, saying that it would be a valuable experience. I followed his suggestion. At the end of the vigil, all went to bed. Three hours later, everyone was up again, to attend the liturgy, which lasted an hour and three quarters.

These services leave one exhausted. After attending them, a layman comes to appreciate fully the popular Greek saying: «Monastic life is very arduous» *(Vareia einai e kalogeriki)*. Father Gabriel informed me that there are more than fifty vigil services a year, and that they are found very exhausting by the younger monks, but less so by the older ones. Evidently, monastic discipline increases one's power to stay awake and to endure extreme bodily discomfort.

The main and direct purpose of these long services is, of course, to worship God or to honor a certain saint. However, from my study of the Scriptures and the writings of the Eastern Fathers, my talks with monks, and my own experience, it is clear to me that such vigils are designed also to promote inner wakefulness or attention, and to produce certain physical effects that are conducive to inner development. They cause extreme discomfort and fatigue by compelling one to stand still for hours in a cramped stall, and therefore require and gradually develop great patience and will-power. These vigils are in accordance with Christ's injunction: «Be wakeful *(gregorete)* and pray, that you may not enter into temptation» (Matt. 26: 41); and with St. Paul's: «I harass *(ypopiazo)* my body, and bring it under subjection, lest after preaching to others, I myself should be a castaway» (1 Cor. 9: 26).

One can learn a great deal about the steadfastness, serenity, and austerity of Orthodoxy by taking part in such services.

During my stay at Dionysiou, I had many talks with Fathers Gabriel and Theocletos. Among the themes I discussed at length with Gabriel was the daily schedule of this

MONASTERY OF DIONYSIOU
South side

KATHOLIKON OF DIONYSIOU
View of nave, showing iconostasis, icon stands, corona, etc.

monastery. He said the following with regard to it:

«At this time of the year, [fall], we rise at six o'clock Byzantine time, that is, six hours after sunset, and pray in private for an hour. At seven, we go to the *katholikon* for the *orthros,* which takes from two to three hours. Then we return to our cells and sleep for two hours. At twelve, we rise and go to the side chapel of the main church for the liturgy and a prayer of entreaty *(paraklesis)*. (On Sundays and major holy days the liturgy is performed in the *katholikon* proper.) These take about an hour and a half. When they are over, we go to the refectory and have our first meal, which takes about half an hour. During the next two hours, between two and six, we occupy ourselves with our special tasks. Next we have a two hour period of rest and study, followed by an hour and a half devoted to our tasks. From nine thirty to ten thirty we have vespers in

REFECTORY OF DIONYSIOU
Pulpit in the center, reading stand in the foreground

the main church. Then we eat supper. After this, we take a walk for half an hour. At twelve, when the gate of the monastery closes, we have the *apodeipnon,* which takes about thirty minutes. At one o'clock, which is one hour after sunset, we go to bed.

«This schedule,» he went on, «holds for the spring and fall on Tuesdays, Thursdays, and Saturdays. It is different during the other seasons and also on Sundays, Mondays, Wednesdays, Fridays, major holy days and days when there are all-night services, and during the long periods of fasting. I will explain. In the summer the *orthros* starts, by Byzantine time, at seven thirty, while in the winter it starts at eight. The time of the liturgy alters according to these changes, and so does that of other things on our program. The time of the vespers and the *apodeipnon,* however, remains fixed. Throughout the year, the vesper service starts at nine thirty and the *apodeipnon* at twelve, except the *great apodeipnon,* which we have only during Lent: this starts at ten thirty. On Sundays and major holy days, the *orthros* takes four to five hours. On Mondays, Wednesdays and Fridays, and during the fasting periods, instead of two meals, one after the liturgy and the other after the vespers, we have a single meal, served at five o'clock, that is, towards noon. The morning meal is replaced by a cup of Turkish coffee.»

Summing up his account, Father Gabriel said:

«Our typical day thus comprises roughly eight hours of prayer, eight of work, and eight of rest.»

What are the conditions for joining this brotherhood? I put this question to Gabriel, and he gave the following reply:

«To become a monk here, one has to be a novice from one to three years. During this period, one must conform absolutely to all the rules of the monastery, following its program, attending regularly the church services, partaking of the same food as the others and nothing beyond this, and obeying strictly his superiors.»

With Father Theocletos I talked about certain other matters pertaining to monasticism. Theocletos seems to be in his early forties and has been at the monastery for twelve years. Although he has received only a high school education, he has a very disciplined mind and has written many fine articles for religious periodicals, and two books. In our talks, he spoke with clarity, good sense, and great facility, without having to pause for the right word or formula. He showed considerable erudition, making reference to many writers, including Augustine, Aquinas, Anselm, Kant, Bergson, Freud, Nicodemos the Aghiorite, and Kierkegaard. As a theologian, he impressed me as being one of the best in Greece today.

Although gifted, Theocletos has no illusions about

IN THE REFECTORY
Archimandrite Gabriel at the center

himself, and is not a proud man. As one who lives in a monastery, he places himself far below the true hermit.

«A monastery,» he said, «is a school for children, as far as the spiritual life is concerned.»

«You are employing the word children in the symbolic sense it has in the Scriptures,» I remarked. «To be a child in this sense is no small achievement.»

«I have in mind especially the sense in which St. Paul employs it in his Epistle to the Galatians, where he depicts the state of being a ‹child› as not being one of supreme fulfilment, but as representing a lower stage of spiritual development. He says: ‹The heir, as long as he is a child, differeth nothing from a servant, though he be lord of all; but is under tutors and governors until the time appointed of the father› (4:1-2). A monastery is a school where men are instructed and trained in the science and art of purifying themselves of what the Church Fathers call passions. (That is, bad thoughts, negative emotions, vices). Those who have achieved such purification are qualified to become hermits. A hermit has the possibility of rising to the state of contemplation *(theoria)*, of mystical union with God.»

«But isn't mystical experience possible to those who live in monasteries?» I asked.

«No,» he replied. «To attain to such an experience one must live in complete quiet *(esychia)* and pray constantly. But one who lives in a monastery is burdened with cares and tasks that make this impossible.»

«Are there mystics on Mount Athos today?» I asked Theocletos.

«Yes,» he answered, «among the hermits. Of course, the fact that one is a hermit does not mean that one is necessarily a mystic *(theoretikos)*.»

Like Modestos of the Monastery of Constamonitou, Theocletos stressed the need of a spiritual guide for one's spiritual health and development. He holds that even mental prayer is dangerous if practiced without the guidance of such a person.

«This form of prayer,» he said, «is a challenge to the powers of evil; it arouses them fiercely against us, and we must know how to engage successfully in ‹spiritual warfare› against them. Apart from a competent spiritual guide there is the danger of going astray, of losing one's reason.»

I asked him what he thought of the *Philokalia* and whether he recommended it for laymen. Like the other monks with whom I had talked about this work, Theocletos expressed very high esteem for it. But he asserted that one cannot practice its teachings while in «the world.»

«The *Philokalia* requires life in monastic seclusion,» he said, «and leads to it.»

He did not mean to deny that there is much in this work that can be adopted and utilized by a layman who is intelligent, sincere, and has a good spiritual guide, but rather that it is only in a monastic establishment that its

FRESCO, KATHOLIKON OF DIONYSIOU

teachings can be fully and most effectively applied.

In addition to my conversations with the monks, I found the study of the main church, the refectory, and the library of the monastery very rewarding. The esonarthex and the nave of the church, which is built in the very narrow courtyard, are decorated with excellent frescoes that were painted by the Cretan iconographer Tzortzis in 1547, the year the church was rebuilt, after it had been destroyed by fire in 1535. These frescoes are comparable to those of the Monastery of Lavra, both being works of the Cretan School.

Besides the murals, the *katholikon* has some excellent panel icons also done in the true Byzantine style. Especially noteworthy are five large panels in the sanctuary, depicting Peter, the Virgin Mary, Christ, John the Baptist, and Paul. They are mounted on the iconostasis, facing eastward, in the order in which I have listed them, and thus constitute a Great Deësis. These icons were done in 1542 by a priest named Eufrosynos.

The walls of the refectory, too, are all adorned with frescoes. These were painted in 1547 and 1615. Some of them are very outstanding, but most of them lack technical finesse and sublimity of the frescoes in the *katholikon.* The one that especially attracted my attention was the large (10 feet wide and 16½ feet high), very well preserved, sixteenth century composition representing symbolically the basic idea of St. John Climacos' *Ladder,* which explains how a monk may rise progressively, through thirty virtues, to spiritual perfection. In this composition there is a ladder with thirty rungs that is fixed on the earth and reaches to heaven. The ladder is made up of two equal parts that rise at different angles. The lower half rises at an angle of about forty-five degrees, while the upper half goes up vertically, showing that the higher levels of spiritual development call for greater efforts and are more difficult to attain. On the ladder there are monks at various stages of ascent. To the left of the ladder, demons—representing evil or negative inner factors, as well as actual beings — are

THE LADDER OF ST. JOHN CLIMACOS
Fresco, refectory of Dionysiou

seeking to thwart the ascent of the monks and succeed in causing some of them to fall, while to the right of the ladder, good angels — representing good or positive inner factors and good practices, as well as actual beings — encourage and assist the monks in their upward movement.

«... The stars of the sky fell to the earth... and every one... hid in the caves and among the rocks of the Mountains;... »

(Rev. 6: 13-15)

Fresco, cloister of the refectory, Dionysiou

« . . . From the pit rose smoke like the smoke of a great furnace . . . . Then from the smoke came locusts on the earth. . . like horses arrayed for battle; . . . »

Rev. 9: 2-7

Fresco, cloister of the refectory, Dionysiou

A monk who has fallen from the ladder, over to the left side, is being swallowed by a huge dragon below, and two others who also have fallen from the same side are on the way to the gaping mouth of the monster, which represents Hell. An elderly monk has reached the top of the ladder and is being crowned by Christ, Who emerges from Heaven.

Another fresco that arrested my attention was in the cloister before the refectory and is inspired by the Book of Revelation 6: 12-17. In this painting is depicted a city with peculiar thick clouds above it and what appear to be stars or exploding bombs falling down from the sky and destroying the buildings. It the foreground are people who have sought refuge in caves. Although this painting was done in 1635, one could easily take it for an imaginative representation by a contemporary painter showing a city under airplane bombardment, with its inhabitants in air raid shelters. The monks regard it as a prophecy of such bombings.

Still another fresco that made me stop and examine it closely was one near the preceding composition and done by the same iconographer. It shows locust-like creatures with human heads, iron-like arms, wings, and long cloud-like tails. These creatures fly at various altitudes around a big mushroom-like cloud that rises out of a pit. Scattered about lie dead human bodies. This fresco is inspired by the Book of Revelation chapter 9, and interpreted by the monks as follows: The locust-like creatures symbolize jet-propelled airplanes; the mushroom-like cloud symbolizes the clouds formed by the explosion of atomic bombs, and the dead men are those who will die from wars involving such planes and bombs.

The library of Dionysiou is housed in two rooms, one above the other, in the big, tall tower of defense. In the upper room are kept the manuscripts, first editions, and older books in general, while in the lower room are kept modern and foreign language books, and periodicals, chiefly religious. There are eight hundred and four manuscripts. These have been carefully catalogued and are kept neatly in glass-doored bookcases. The oldest is a sixth century parchment Book of the Gospels written in capitals. A significant feature of this manuscript, which is well-preserved despite its age, is the presence of musical signs *(symadophona)* under the words. No one has been able to find the key to these signs. But their presence in this work is clear evidence that the practice which is observed in Orthodox churches today of intoning the Gospel passages goes at least as far back as the sixth century. Among the other especially noteworthy manuscripts are two Books of the Gospels, dating one from the tenth and the other from the eleventh century. These are decorated with designs and icons of the rarest beauty, and are unique on Mount Athos.

MONASTERY OF GRIGORIOU

Continuing my journey, I went by rowboat to the next monastery northwestward, Grigoriou. The boat belonged to the Monastery of Dionysiou and was rowed by a layman. I was let off at the fine little harbor of Grigoriou,

MONASTERY OF GRIGORIOU

and walked uphill to the monastery, which is a short distance away, built on a rock that is washed by the sea.

Grigoriou was founded in the thirteenth or fourteenth century, but has been destroyed twice, first by pirates in 1500 and then by fire in 1761. As a result, its buildings and paintings are relatively new. The main church has disappointing modern frescoes, while the refectory has none.

I did not see the abbot, Archimandrite Bessarion, who is reputed to be an excellent administrator, as he happened to be away. The monk who acted as my guide told me that Bessarion studied medicine at the University of Athens, but left before finishing his studies, at the end of his third year.

Like the other monasteries on Mount Athos, Grigoriou has had better days. In 1920, for instance, it had sixty-six monks, not counting novices, whereas today it has only about forty monks and five or six novices, and is confronted with serious financial difficulties it did not have then. The financial difficulties which this and the other Athonite monasteries face today arise in large measure from the fact that in 1926 the Greek goverment, confronted with the staggering problem of supporting a million and a half Greeks who were expelled from Asia Minor by the Turks during 1921-23, took over most of the monasteries' land estates (*metochia*) that were outside the Mountain. Although the State undertook to compensate the monasteries annually, it has not been able in recent years fully to carry out its commitments, owing to the enormous economic difficulties that beset it as a result of the great destruction that was caused during the Second World War by the Italians, Germans, and Bulgarians, and by the communist revolution that followed. Thus, in 1953 it gave to the monasteries only twenty per cent of the money it used to give them prior to the Second World War.

Among the monks at Grigoriou with whom I had occasion to converse was Theodore Cakounes, one of the elders close to the abbot. Father Theodore was delighted to learn that I was from Boston.

«I have lived near Boston, in Lynn, for three and a half years,» he said. «I worked for General Electric, with one of my brothers who is now a monk at Kapsokalyvia. He stayed in Lynn longer. I left Lynn in 1905 and came directly to the Holy Mountain. A few years later, he followed my example. I have two more brothers, both of them in America. When I came to the Holy Mountain, I was only nineteen years old. I came here resolved to become a monk, and I have stuck to my resolution.»

«What led you to make such a choice, and gave you such firmness of purpose?» I asked.

«It was the Grace of God,» he replied, «that called me and gave me the power.»

«How do you find monastic life?»

«I like it very much. If I were to return to the age of nineteen, I would choose this life again.»

«It is often said that the monastic life is grievous,» I remarked.

«The life of a monk,» Theodore replied, «*is* grievous *if* it is taken the *wrong* way. But if it is taken in the *right* spirit, it is very easy to bear. I mean, if a monk has an intense love for God and gives primacy to spiritual values, his austere mode of life becomes for him easy and joyful.»

What Theodore said was confirmed by his presence. He radiated inward peace and true joy, thus providing an excellent commentary on Christ's statement, «My yoke is easy and my burden is light» (Matt. 11:30).

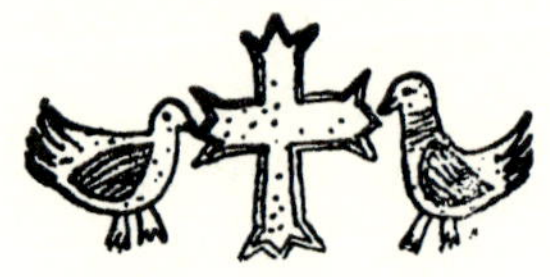

MONASTERY OF SIMONOPETRA

From the Monastery of Grigoriou I proceeded further northwestward to that of Simonos Petra, or Simonopetra, as the monks of Athos usually call it. The two monasteries are not far from one another. Simonopetra can be reached

MONASTERY OF SIMONOPETRA

from Grigoriou either by walking the whole distance, over difficult terrain, or by taking a boat to the *arsanas* of Simonopetra and walking the rest of the distance. The guest-master of Grigoriou asked one of the workmen to take me to Simonopetra's *arsanas* in Grigoriou's rowboat. When we reached the *arsanas,* I got off at the pier and walked up the steep, stone-paved, zigzag path. I arrived at Simonopetra after half an hour's walk amidst very rich vegetation. During my walk I looked with awe at the seven-storied buildings of the monastery above me. The high, isolated, tower-like rock on which they are built greatly accentuates their height and renders the monastery the most striking construction on Athos. The west side is the most impressive, and it is this that one sees from the sea or as one approaches the monastery from the pier.

The buildings that make up Simonopetra are all new, yet definitely Byzantine in style. Since its foundation about the middle of the fourteenth century, the whole monastery has been destroyed by fire thrice—in 1581, in 1635, and in 1891. Only the sacred relics and a few other things were saved from the last fire. In the *katholikon* one will see no wall paintings. The library consists of a single small room containing only printed books, nearly all of them new.

Simonopetra is coenobitic. It has about twenty-five monks, most of them Greeks from Asia Minor. I had occasion to converse with several of them, and found them very friendly and devout.

This was the last monastery I visited during my 1954 sojourn on Athos.

SERBIAN MONASTERY OF HILANDARI

I revisited Mount Athos in May, 1958. From Thessaloniki to Ierissos my trip followed the same pattern as in 1954. At Ierissos, however, instead of taking the bus to Trypiti and the motorboat from there to the port of Daphne, I took the motorboat to Hilandari, the Serbian monastery, on the northeast side of the Athos peninsula. My plan was to visit all the monasteries on this side of the peninsula that I had not visited before, as well as those that I had, and to turn around the tip of the peninsula and visit as many of the monastic establishments on the other side as time permitted.

The sea was calm on the day of my arrival in Ierissos, and the captain of the motorboat that leaves from here assured me and the other travelers who were thinking of following this route that the sea would be quiet the next day, too. And indeed it was. The boat left Ierissos early in the morning, at six, and proceeded first to the village of Nea Roda, half an hour away, and then to the *arsanas* of Hilandari, which is the first Athonite port on this side of the peninsula. As it moved away from Nea Roda, several dolphins made their appearance just ahead of us, rising and diving.

The boat arrived at the port of Hilandari within three hours after its departure from Ierissos. The monastery itself is about three quarters of an hour from the port and is not visible from it. I walked there with one of the monks of Hilandari who had come here for some matter and was returning to the monastery. He was a tall, genial Serb who spoke Greek.

A short distance from the beach, near a big medieval tower, the monk led me off the main road to a spring with cool, delicious water, which he said was *aghiasma,* holy water. We both had a drink, and without tarrying long resumed our walk.

From my conversation with my companion, I learned that he was named Domitian and that he came to Mount Athos thirty-seven years ago, after serving in the army. He came as a pilgrim, liked the Holy Mountain very much, and decided to stay here.

Domitian asked me my name, nationality, and profession, and about economic, social, and other conditions in the United States. Our conversation then turned to the Monastery of Hilandari.

«How many monks are there at your monastery?» I asked Domitian.

«About twenty-five,» he replied. «The number has been growing smaller with years. When I came, there were eighty-five.»

«Are they all from Yugoslavia?» I asked.

«No; there are also three or four Russians,» he answered.

«What do you think has been causing the drop in the number of monks?»

«I believe,» said Domitian, «that the reason for this is the fact that men today do not find life on Athos satisfying. Life in the world has changed much since I came here. The diet has changed, gadgets have increased, making life easier and pleasanter. Men come to Athos, become novices, put on the cassock, but after a few months they leave, return to the world. Life on Athos involves much suffering, arising from the great quietness of the place, the monotony of life, the plainness of the diet, the repeated fasts, the long daily church services.»

«What has enabled you to endure such suffering for so many years, and not flee back to the world?» I asked.

«We read the Gospels and the Apostle Paul. We keep

ST. JOHN CHRYSOSTOM PRAYING
Fresco, katholikon of Hilandari

remembering what suffering our Lord Himself went through, and we endure everything. Also, we read the Fathers. We read all of them, either in Greek or in translation.»

«What about men who live in the world?» I asked. «They live so differently from you. Do you see any hope for them?»

«In the world, too,» replied Domitian, «there are many

persons who are as good as monks. It is not the cassock by itself that makes the monk.»

Our discussion turned to the religious services at Hilandari.

«In what language,» I asked Domitian, «are the services at your monastery performed?»

«In Slavonic,» he replied. «It's the same with the Bulgarians and Russians. But we perform them in Greek when we have Greek dignitaries. In conversation among ourselves, however, we Serbs use the Serbian language, which is a newer form of the Slavonic.»

As we were walking, I noticed a wire that apparently ran from the *arsanas* to the monastery, and I asked Domitian what it was.

«That's a telephone wire,» he said, «which connects the *arsanas* with the monastery. It's a good thing, a big convenience.»

«I see. Life after all *is* changing here somewhat,» I remarked.

«We now have a tractor, too,» added Domitian. «It was sent as a gift to our monastery by Premier Tito. He also sent us an electric generator to provide the monastery with electric lighting.»

«So you have electric lighting now!»

«Well, actually we only use the generator for a month or two in the winter, when the nights are very long, and on major holidays and when we receive dignitaries, provided we can find someone who knows how to operate it. It's noisy; and besides, we cannot afford to pay a mechanic to service it throughout the year.»

When we reached Hilandari, which lies in a richly vegetated valley amidst low hills, Father Domitian took me first to the refectory, west of the *katholikon,* and then to the guesthouse nearby. The refectory is a large oblong building that has seats for about one hundred and fifty monks. Its walls are covered in the interior with old frescoes having Slavonic inscriptions. As Hilandari is idiorrhythmic, the refectory is not used, except on certain holy days, thrice a year.

Domitian expressed sorrow that the monastery was idiorrhythmic, and praised the coenobitie monasteries, especially Dionysiou and Constamonitou, as having a stricter, severer mode of life than the idiorrhythmic.

MONASTERY OF HILANDARI

«But God is very benevolent,» he said, «and He will save us, too.»

I have heard other monks, both in idiorrhythmic and in coenobitic monasteries, strongly disapprove of the idiorrhythmic system and express their earnest desire that the nine idiorrhythmic monasteries of Athos return to the coenobitic system. They consider idiorrhythmism a deviation of monastic life that damages the monasteries both financially and spiritually. They stress that the older form of monastic organization, the coenobitic, benefits the monasteries in both respects: it cuts down expenses and frees the monks from many unnecessary cares, producing a more peaceful state of mind, and leaving more time for study and prayer.

The guestmaster is a middle-aged, slender Serbian monk named Zossima. He is very polite, dignified, intelligent, and speaks excellent Greek with an unusually clear enunciation. He provided me with first rate hospitality and gave me some useful data about Hilandari. After one of the vesper services, he took me about the *katholikon* and showed me the tomb of St. Symeon, the former Serbian ruler Stephen Nemanya, who gave up his throne, withdrew to Mount Athos, and with his son, St. Savvas, founded the monastery towards the end of the twelfth century. He also showed me a famous large, very old panel icon of the Holy Virgin, called Panaghia Triherousa and said to have belonged to St. John Damascene. It is a remarkable specimen of Byzantine art, full of austere spiritual beauty. The *katholikon* was built in 1293 by Stephen Milutin, and was frescoed in the fourteenth century.

CHRIST TEACHING
Fresco, katholikon of Hilandari

I asked Father Zossima about the music they employ in the church services.

«It doesn't sound Byzantine to me,» I said, as we were having supper on a balcony of the guesthouse overlooking a large vegetable garden below. «The manner in which the voice is produced is Western, and there is no *isocratema*» (drone or holding-tone).

«You are right,» he said. «It is not Byzantine. It's Serbian, with a European basis.»

«It is not like the music the Russian monks use,» I went on to say.

«No, no,» remarked Zossima. The Russians employ four-part music, and must have four voices in order to execute it properly. But we don't have part music.»

The library of Hilandari is housed in a small chapel. According to the librarian, Father Savvas—a kind and cheerful elderly Serb who speaks Greek fluently—it comprises about six hundred Slavonic and one hundred Greek manuscripts, and about seven thousand printed books.

In a room adjacent to the library are contained a number of remarkable icons done in the Byzantine style. Among them is an eleventh century mosaic on a panel, depicting the Holy Virgin and Child, and ten large panel icons, probably dating from the end of the sixteenth century, depicting Matthew, Luke, Mark, Peter, John the Theologian, Paul, John the Baptist, the Holy Virgin, and the Archangels Michael and Gabriel.

Another, larger collection of panel icons is kept in a spacious oblong room. These icons are of different dates and styles, and of widely varying artistic merit. In this room are also to be seen several large embroidered compositions that were made in Serbia. Among them is one that was made and presented to the monastery by Efimia (14th century), wife of the Serbian ruler Ouglessa, and that was used as a curtain for the Beautiful Gate.

MONASTERY OF ESPHIGMENOU

From Hilandari I proceeded to Esphigmenou, the next monastery on the northeastern side of the Athos peninsula. The first half of the road to Esphigmenou is the same as

MONASTERY OF ESPHIGMENOU

that which leads to the *arsanas* of the Serbian monastery. At a certain point one takes a mule path to the right, and after about fifteen minutes' walk he arrives at Esphigmenou, close by the sea.

On the way, I took notice of the landscape and the

sounds. I was especially struck by the luxuriant, tall grass that covered the plains and slopes, the abundance of white, blue, yellow, and red flowers that dotted it, and by the ceaseless humming of bees. This humming and the occasional song of birds were the only sounds I could hear.

Soon after I entered the gate of Esphigmenou's quadrangle of four-storied buildings, I encountered a meek and benign old monk, the porter, at work making a fence for a young lotus tree. He asked me where I was from and what my name was. When I replied, he said:

«May you live! [*Na zisis!* A typical remark of Athonite monks.] So you are from America! I have a brother in New York, and I myself have been in America, in the state of Washington. That was many years ago. I stayed there three years. Then I left America and came here, at the age of thirty. I have been on the Holy Mountain fifty years.

«Your name, Father?» I asked.

«Cornelius,» he replied. «In the world my name was Constantine. But as you probably know, when one becomes a monk he receives a new name, usually one that starts with the same initial letter as the original.»

When we had talked for a while, Cornelius interrupted his work and took me to the guestmaster, Agathangelos, a very friendly monk. Agathangelos offered me a spoonful of quince-jelly, a little cup of coffee, and a glass of cool water. After we had conversed for a time, he showed me to a room on the outer side of the guesthouse, overlooking the sea. I went inside, opened one of the windows, and beheld an uncommonly beautiful view of the sea and coast. Then, as I sat writing, I heard the rhythmic pounding of the waves as they broke on the sturdy foundation blocks that extend into the sea.

After a vespers, one of the monks, named Gerontios,

whom I met as the service was about to start, came over to me while I was in the narthex and said:

«As you seem to be interested in our practices, I would like to explain to you certain things about our life.»

Thereupon he took me to the south side chapel of the *katholikon,* and started describing the nature and sequence of the church services and other practices.

«Everyday,» said Gerontios, «including Sundays, a small bell *(kambanaki)* is rung one hour before the *orthros* starts. It is a notice for the monks to get up. They rise at once and pray for three quarters of an hour in their cells. Each monk does a minimum of one hundred prostrations, and says twelve rosaries *(komboskinia).* A rosary, you know, has a hundred knots. Three rosaries are said to Jesus. At each knot the monk says: ‹Lord Jesus Christ, Son of God, have mercy upon me.› Then the monk says three rosaries to the Holy Virgin, repeating the prayer: ‹Most Holy Theotokos, save us.› Next, one rosary is said to the saint who is celebrated that day, one to all the saints, and one to the saint that has the same name as the monk who is praying. Finally, three more rosaries are said to Jesus.»

Father Gerontios took me out of the *katholikon* and showed me the small bell that is used for waking up the monks, and explained that it is also rung one hour before the liturgy starts and shortly before the vesper service and the meals. This bell hangs from a beam in the porch at the west side of the church.

«The *orthros,*» he went on, «takes from two hours to two and a half. Shortly after the *orthros* comes the liturgy, except on Sundays and holy days, when there is an intermission of one hour. On days preceded by an all-night vigil service, there is an intermission of two hours. The vesper service begins at 9:45 by Byzantine time, while the *apodeipnon* begins at 11:45 by the same time system, except on days when there is going to be an all-night vigil

ST. GREGORY PALAMAS

— it is then performed at the beginning of such a service. The vespers take about three quarters of an hour, while the *apodeipnon* lasts about half an hour.»

«You spoke about the use of the *small* bell,» I said to Gerontios. «What about the *large* bells?»

«The large bells» *(kambanes)* are used only on Sundays and major holy days, to announce the *orthros*, liturgy, and vespers.»

As we were talking, a short, very old and thin monk, named Germanos, approached us and asked me where I was from. Upon learning that I was a Bostonian, he expressed pleasant surprise and said that he himself had lived in Boston, between 1890 and 1892. After that, he explained, he went to Russia and stayed there for about the same period of time. Then he came to this monastery.

Germanos next asked me what my profession was. When I had explained, he remarked slowly and solemnly:

«Good. Very good. But cultivate faith and piety. Without these a man is a plain zero. Our Lord has said: ‹Without me you can do nothing› (John 15:5). Also, whatever you do, keep in mind the supreme aim. Our supreme aim is salvation. Never to anything that is contrary to it.»

The *apodeipnon* was about to start, and we went into the *katholikon*. I recalled reading that a great fourteenth century Byzantine mystic, St. Gregory Palamas, was for a time abbot of this monastery, and I asked Germanos if there was an icon of the saint in the church, and also if any other saints had lived at Esphigmenou. Germanos answered both questions in the affirmative. In connection with the second, he mentioned the names of several saints and added that of course there must have been others, whose names are not preserved. In the exonarthex he showed me a fresco depicting St. Antony Petchersky, a native of Russia, and St. Damian. Proceeding to the *liti*, he showed me frescoes of two other monks of Esphigmenou who had attained sainthood: St. Jacob and St. Agathangelos. Finally, advancing into the main body of the church, he pointed to the icon of St. Gregory Palamas, on the iconostasis.

Although Esphigmenou was founded in the tenth century, the murals of the *katholikon* are not of the Byzantine period, as the monastery was destroyed by fire towards the end of the fifteenth century and by pirates in 1533. They are not outstanding works of art, but they emanate piety. Among those that arrested my attention was the figure of St. Theodosios the Coenobiarch, painted in the nave. This saint holds in his left hand a scroll with the following statement:

«Unless you renounce all worldly things, you cannot become monks.»

Esphigmenou has over three hundred manuscripts and four or five thousand printed books. All the manuscripts and the most valuable printed books are kept in a room above the exonarthex of the *katholikon*. The librarian, a kind elderly monk named Procopios, took me and the other guests to this library and showed us several precious manuscripts, including a large parchment Tetraevangelion (the Four Gospels) of the eleventh century, with superb miniatures of the gospel writers; a monumental eleventh century Menologion (a book containing accounts of martyrdoms) with numerous fine miniatures; and a very large tenth century parchment manuscript containing homilies of St. John Chrysostom on the six days of the Creation.

MONASTERY OF PANTOCRATOROS

From Esphigmenou I went by motorboat to Vatopedi, the next monastery on the northeastern coast of the Athos peninsula as one moves towards the promontory, and from there, again by motorboat, to the next monastery south-

MONASTERY OF PANTOCRATOROS

eastward, Pantocratoros. The distance from Esphigmenou to Vatopedi was covered in half an hour; that from Vatopedi to Pantocratoros, in three quarters of an hour. The sea was quiet.

Pantocratoros has a tiny harbor that is for rowboats

only. The monastery is built on a rocky cliff close by the sea, at a spot that offers a very extensive view of the sea and land. Looking southward, one has a splendid view of Mount Athos rising to its magnificent peak. Looking in the same direction at the coast, one notices about two or three kilometers away the Monastery of Stavronikita. If one turns his gaze westward, one sees up on the slope of a hill the Russian skete of the Prophet Elias, which is a dependency of Pantocratoros.

At the gate the porter stopped me and asked me for my official letter of admission to the monasteries. I answered that I did not have one, and explained how, wishing to make the best use of my time, I had started my journey on Athos from Hilandari, had visited in succession Esphigmenou and Vatopedi, and now that I was near Karyes I was planning to go there the next day, procure my letter of admission and then resume my journey on this side of the peninsula, starting from the next monastery, that of Stavronikita. This satisfied him, and he took me to the guestmaster, who provided me with the customary Athonite hospitality.

Pantocratoros, which was founded about the end of the fourteenth century, is one of the smaller Athonite monasteries. It has only fifteen monks, although it could provide living quarters for many times that number. Its system is idiorrhythmic.

I had occasion to meet and talk with several very pious monks, including the librarian, named Theocletos, who is rather young, apparently in his twenties, and the *typikaris,* Agathangelos, who is about fifty. Theocletos showed me the library, which is housed in a room up in the tower of the monastery and includes, besides printed books, three hundred and eleven manuscripts, among which are several priceless scrolls containing the liturgies of St. Basil and St. John Chrysostom. Father Agathangelos took me about the *katholikon* and showed me various things of special interest. This church was built in 1450, and is dedicated to the Transfiguration of Christ. It has seven domes. Three of these are over the esonarthex — one at the middle of the west side and two at either end of the east side; one, the largest, rising high above the others, is at the center of the main body of the church; two small ones are at the sanctuary — one over the north and one over the south side apse; and one is over the chapel at the north side of the church. The iconostasis has excellent icons, done centuries ago.

One feature of Athonite church services that came vividly to my attention at this monastery was the censing, performed by the officiating priest, a sturdy young man. The lively rattling of the censer, which the priest shook with unusual rapidity and vigor, made me follow the procedure from beginning to end. Starting from the Holy Gate, he went all around the nave and censed separately each and every person there. Then he proceeded into the esonarthex and did the same thing. This practice seems clearly to serve at least two purposes: to arouse the worshippers to a state of inner wakefulness, through the sounds of its little bells, and to elicit in the worshippers a feeling of the sublime, an aspiration for the divine, by bringing the fragrant smell of incense close to every one of them. The incense does to the worshipper, through the sense of smell, what the sacred icon does to him through the sense of sight, and what sacred music does through that of hearing.

CENSER

MONASTERY OF STAVRONIKITA

Leaving Pantocratoros, I went by foot to Karyes, procured my letter of admission, visited the Church of the Protaton, several monks who paint icons, and the nearby Monastery of Koutloumousiou, and then set out for Stavronikita.

Like Pantocratoros, Stavronikita is built on a cliff close by the sea and offers a very extensive view of the sea and land, including the peak of Athos. It is the newest, smallest, and poorest Athonite monastery. It consists of a small quadrangle of two-, three-, and four-storied buildings, with a *katholikon* that stands free on all sides except the south in the little courtyard.

Soon after entering the yard, I met a very devout elderly monk with a ragged cassock. He was the *ecclesiarch* and *typikaris* of the monastery. After asking me the usual questions about my place of origin, name, etc., he accompanied me into the church, which I was interested in seeing.

This church was built between 1540 and 1553, and is the smallest *katholikon* on Athos. It has a single, relatively large narthex, and is topped by two domes, one over the narthex and one over the nave. The dome of the nave is larger than that of the narthex and is set on a higher level. Both divisions of the church are frescoed. The older frescoes of the nave, such as the Pantocrator in the dome, which were done in 1546, are excellent. There are fine panel icons on the iconostasis, and a superb fourteenth century panel mosaic on the icon stand *(proskynitarion)* in the south part of the nave. This mosaic is about a foot wide and over a foot high, and depicts St. Nicholas, to whom the church is dedicated.

After leaving the church, I conversed with the monk for a long time, first in the courtyard and then in his cell, where he had to go to prepare his meal, as the monastery is idiorrhythmic. His name, I learned, is Anthimos. He is a native of Kalamata and has been a monk here for twenty-two years.

«How many monks does Stavronikita have, Father Anthimos?» I asked.

«Only eight,» he answered. «Today young men don't want to become monks. They lack religious fervor. They even dislike religion.»

In his cell, consisting of a single small room, Anthimos made me some coffee. Then he cut and fried squash for his midday meal.

Amongst other things, we discussed the present state of mankind. Anthimos was pessimistic.

«My observations and those of other monks here,» he said, «show that people—men and women, young and old—are moving more and more in the direction of materialism. Their attention has been shifting steadily away from the soul and God, to the external, material world; away from the eternal and imperishable, to the temporal and corruptible. One of the major causes of this is science. The ‹great conquests› of science, the latest instances of which are the atomic bomb and the satellites, increase man's pride and cause him to put his trust in his own devices and in matter rather than in God.»

I noticed half a dozen books in Anthimos' cell, and this led me to ask him what works he especially recommended. Thereupon he picked up Nikephoros Theotokis' *Book of the Sunday Gospel Passages* and said:

«This is a very good work. It contains all the Gospel excerpts that are read in church on Sundays, and illuminating interpretations of them. In the past, such books were widely read. Today, unfortunately, people do not read

MONASTERY OF STAVRONIKITA

the Holy Scriptures. They read instead newspapers and fiction. But newspapers are a deception: they say one thing today and the opposite tomorrow; while works of fiction usually corrupt instead of improving the soul. The *Philokalia,* too, is a fine book. Also Nicodemos' *Garden of Graces* and *The Unseen Warfare* are very good. Dukakis'

Great Collection of Lives of Saints (Megas Synaxaristis), too, is extremely good.»

(The last mentioned work of fourteen volumes was compiled and edited by Constantine Dukakis (1840-1908), who spent some time on Mount Athos, and was published between 1889 and 1897.)

MONK STRIKINC WOODEN SEMANTRON

Later in the day, while I was walking about the courtyard, studying the architecture of the main church and the other buildings, I saw Anthimos striking the wooden *semantron* for the vespers. When he was through, he approached me and asked:

«Do you know the significance of this practice?»

«Someone has explained it to me,» I replied, «but I would like to hear *your* explanation.»

«Well, according to a popular tradition,» said Anthimos, «this practice goes back to Noah. It is said that Noah used the *semantron* to call the animals into the Ark, and thus save then from the Deluge; and that following his example, we employ it to call the monks into the church, which is a spiritual Ark, in order that they might be saved from the deluge of sin.»

I have heard this explanation from other Athonite

monks, and another one according to which this practice is a reminder of Christ's injunction to cultivate one's talents (Matt. 25: 14-30), as the sounds produced by the *semantron* when it is struck at the peculiar Athonite rhythm resemble the utterance, «*To talanton, to talanton, to tala—tala—talanton,*» thereby reminding the monks of Christ's injunction to cultivate their talents, to strive to grow spiritually by waking up and praying. Underlying both explanations is the same general idea, that of going to church and praying, to assist in the process of their salvation. The first of these interpretations, however, refers to the negative aspect of salvation—deliverance from sin, that is, from wrong thoughts, wrong feelings, wrong deeds; while the second refers to the positive aspect: the development of one's higher potentialities.

The conception of the church as an Ark, in the explanation given by Anthimos, is closely related to St. John Chrysostom's comparison of it to a harbor. «A church,» says Chrysostom, «is a spiritual harbor of souls.... Should a person present in a church open up his conscience, he will find in it great calm. He is neither disturbed by anger, nor driven by despair, nor corrupted by the passion of vanity—all of these wild beasts have subsided, as by some Divine spell» (Migne, *P.G.*, 49, 363).

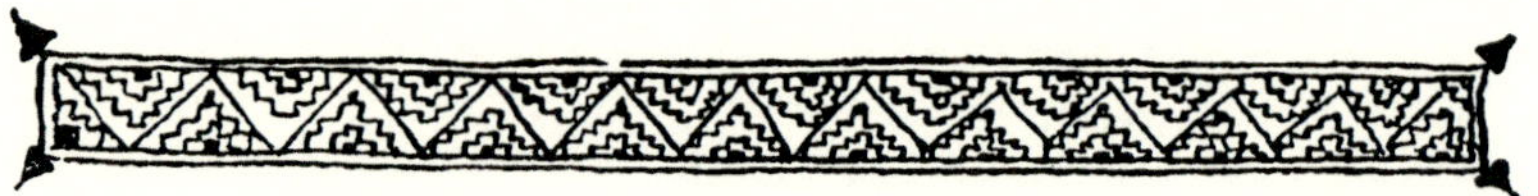

MYLOPOTAMOS

From Stavronikita I walked to the Monastery of Iviron, which is about half an hour southward, with the intention of spending a day or so there and then resuming my journey on this side of the peninsula to the Monastery of Philotheou. When I arrived at Iviron, however, I found it necessary to change my plans. The guestmaster told me that a hundred guests, members of a religious organization, were expected to arrive any minute and that it would be impossible for the monastery to provide me with a bed and other normal hospitality.

«Our monastery,» he said, «has only thirty-six beds for guests. We can provide enough food for everybody, but we are at a loss as to what to do with so many people in the matter of sleep. Most of them will have to sleep on the floor or out in the courtyard. Also, with so many persons here, it won't be possible to really see anything or to converse with us. I suggest therefore that you go to Mylopotamos, stay there for the night and return here after a day or two, when these guests will have left. Mylopotamos is only half an hour's walk from here and the monks there are very clean and hospitable.»

My chief interest in revisiting Iviron was to see Father Athanasios, the librarian. Upon inquiring about him, I learned that he was ill and could not receive any visitors. This fact, together with the crowded conditions that were soon to be created by the mass invasion of guests, made

ST. JOHN CLIMACOS

me leave Iviron after a short stay and proceed to Mylopotamos.

Mylopotamos is a *kelli* that belongs to the Monastery of Lavra. Its conspicuous location on a rock at the tip of a promontory and its tower of defense make it look from a distance like a small monastery. Like Pantocratoros and Stavronikita, it has a wonderful view.

As I opened the gate, a bell connected to it rang, notifying the monks inside of my arrival. Presently, a monk of about twenty-five appeared and led me upstairs to a big porch overlooking the sea. Here two older monks greeted me and asked me to sit down. After explaining my reasons for visiting the Holy Mountain and answering a few questions as to my background, I started enquiring about their *kelli*. I talked mostly with Father Emmanuel, a middle-aged Cretan priest-monk who is the head of this brotherhood, which consists of five monks. Emmanuel is the eldest of the group and looks very calm, meek, and saintly.

«Mylopotamos,» he said, «was founded in the tenth century by St. Athanasios the Athonite. We do not have a full account of its history through the centuries, but it is known to have served at times as a place of exile for eminent church figures, including the Ecumenical Patriarch Gregory V (1745-1821), who stayed here for several years, the Ecumenical Patriarch Joachim III, who lived here for twelve years (1889-1901), and a bishop of Florina, who dwelt here for three years (1917-20). In the recent decades Mylopotamos remained for some time uninhabited. When we came, the buildings were in a very poor state. We leased the *kelli* for fifteen years, at the rate of two hundred okas of olive oil per year, and made the buildings habitable.»

«What are your means of support?» I asked Father Emmanuel.

«We live chiefly by agriculture,» he replied. «Occasionally we do construction work at the monasteries, as we are skilled in building.»

«I suppose your system is similar to that of the coenobitic monasteries,» I remarked.

«Yes», he said. «We have everything in common, we eat together, and worship together in our chapel. The only difference as far as worship is concerned is that we don't have a liturgy every day, but only on Sundays and holy days. The reason for this is that on weekdays we have to work out in the fields for many hours, or to engage in other manual labor away from the *kelli,* whereas the monks in the monasteries spend most of their time inside the monasteries and have more time free from work.»

«How come you chose this form of monasticism?» I asked.

«We prefer it,» he answered, «because it is the ‹royal road,› avoiding both the large number of monks of a monastery, which often gives rise to friction, and the other extreme of a single monk. As regards the latter, Holy Scripture says: ‹Woe to him that is alone when he falls, and there is not a second one to lift him up› » (Eccl. 4: 10).

This answer is quite reminiscent of what St. John Climacos says in his *Ladder.* In the concluding part of his chapter «Concerning Flight from the World», he says: «The whole monastic way of life is divided into three very general kinds of seclusion: striving spiritually in the wilderness all by oneself; living in quiet seclusion with one or two others; and dwelling patiently in a coenobium. ‹Turn not to the right hand nor to the left,› says the Ecclesiastes, but walk in the royal road; for the middle one of the aforementioned ways has proved to be the one that is suitable for most persons. Regarding him who is alone he says, ‹woe to him, for if he falls› into indifference or inner sleep, or indolence, or despair, ‹there is no man to lift him up.› While ‹where two or three are gathered together in my name, there am I in the midst of them,› says the Lord» (Migne, *P. G.*, 88, 641, 644).

MONASTERY OF PHILOTHEOU

Nearly an hour's walk from Mylopotamos, about seven hundred meters (2,296 ft.) above sea level, is the Monastery of Philotheou. It is reached by a steep cobbled path that begins a short distance from the beach at Mylopotamos. I made this monastery my next destination.

As I was approaching it, I was delighted to see an abundance of water running in narrow rivulets at the sides of the road. None of the monasteries on Athos suffer a lack of water, but Philotheou is among those that are especially well supplied the year round.

When I arrived, I was taken by a young monk to the guestmaster, Father Damian. Noticing that my clothes were soaked with perspiration, Damian immediately gave me a room in the guesthouse where I changed my clothes and rested. One perspires a great deal on the Holy Mountain during such journeys in the late spring, the summer and early fall. Walking along the steep and rugged paths is fatiguing, especially since the temperature and humidity are high, and there is usually little or no breeze.

Philotheou is built on a small plateau with mountains to the north and west which are covered with luxuriant forests largely consisting of firs. Although it is far from the sea, one can enjoy the sight of it from the east side of the quadrangle.

The system of this monastery is idiorrhythmic. At present it has twenty-six monks. Damian told me that its financial condition is good. He attributed this to the fact that the forests of Philotheou, from which it derives the greater part of its income, are among the best on Athos.

The main church stands free at the center of the courtyard. According to an epigraph above the central door of the nave, it was built in 1746 and was frescoed in 1752. The murals and panel icons are basically in the Byzantine

MONASTERY OF PHILOTHEOU

tradition, but lack the simplicity and spiritual grandeur of the older icons. Architecturally this building is similar to the older Athonite *katholika,* but it has a striking Western feature over the middle of the narthex—a tall, pointed bell tower. This is out of harmony with the form of the rest of the church, which is topped by five domes.

Although the *katholikon* dates from the eighteenth century, the monastery itself was founded in the tenth, by a monk named Philotheos.

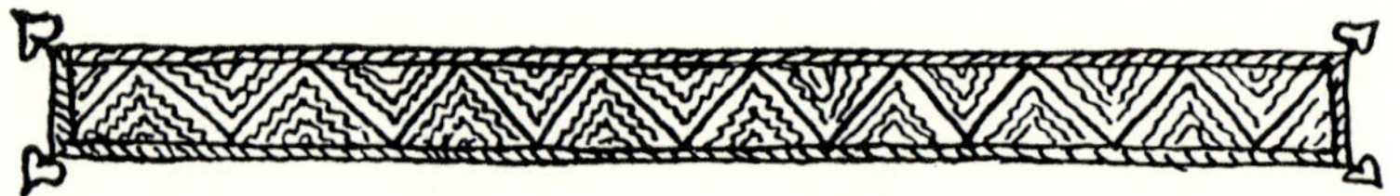

MONASTERY OF KARAKALLOU

The Monastery of Karakallou lies in a valley at a considerably lower altitude than Philotheou, about half an hour's walk southeastward. My trip there was easy and

MONASTERY OF KARAKALLOU

pleasant, as the road is downhill and goes through interesting scenery and very rich vegetation.

It is not known who the founders of this monastery were, but it seems to have been established in the eleventh century. Its *katholikon* has been destroyed by fire three times. The present church was built between 1548 and 1563.

Its sanctuary and nave were decorated with frescoes in 1717, its *liti* in 1750, and the narthex in 1767. These frescoes belong to the Macedonian School of iconography.

Looking at the church from the west side, I noticed a bell tower that rose above the middle of the narthex. It reminded me of the one I had seen at Philotheou.

Karakallou is coenobitic. It has at present thirty-five monks and five novices. This number is not small, considering how many monks there are at other much larger Athonite monasteries. The abbot, Archimandrite Paul, is highly esteemed, not only here, but also elsewhere on Athos and by people outside it. He is one of the most outstanding personalities of the Holy Mountain today.

Paul was not at the monastery when I visited it, but I had the good fortune of meeting him at Thessaloniki the day before my departure for Athos. When I learned that he had come to the hotel where I was staying, I went to see him. He is a good-looking man of about seventy, with a well rounded face, blue eyes, grey hair and a heavy grey beard. His facial expression and bearing are characterized by dignity, without pride or pretense. He speaks with restraint in a quiet voice. Earlier in the year he had delivered a lecture at the Institute for Macedonian Studies. I did not attend this lecture, as I happened to be in Athens at the time, but I had the opportunity of reading it. Paul had taken it with him when he revisited Thessaloniki, with the intention of giving it to some periodical for publication, and he had the kindness to let me borrow it.

In this lecture, he deals with Athonite monasticism in general—its aims, its achievements, its present state. Monasticism for him is «the most perfect expression of the spirituality of the Gospels.» Regarding Athonite monasticism, he says that «its great aim was and is of course preeminently the salvation of the soul. This was achieved and is being achieved through a special organization and system of rules and regulations. Prayer, fasting, love, and common worship were the primary means through which the monks stabilized the beginnings of monastic life.... They sought to simplify life, to achieve inner purity, to develop firm principles of common action or, if you wish, of common property, in their struggle for virtue and coenobitic harmony, and to realize in Jesus Christ, as far as possible more truly, the Kingdom of the Heavenly Father on earth.» On Mount Athos, he goes on to say, «human nature developed all its higher qualities, and struggled to cast off all its defects.»

Why is it that the number of monks on the Mountain has been decreasing in recent times? The abbot's answer is as follows:

«The cause of this phenomenon is chiefly outside Athos, and quite secondarily inside Athos, too. That is, the many and man-destroying wars our nation has had to engage in since 1912, which included two world wars, and the slackening of morals that has resulted from them, have checked, as it seems, at least for a time, the pious disposition towards the monastic life. In addition, although «from the very beginning of its establishment the monastic life has been severe, in our time this mode of life has become even more arduous relatively to secular life, because the latter has become easier and more effortless.... The monks of the Holy Mountain follow the same austere way of life throughout the year. This exhausts novices and usually causes them to return to their former life in the world.»

Is the Holy Mountain then doomed? No. Father Paul believes that the decrease in the number of monks on Athos is a passing phenomenon, and that the disposition for the monastic life will in due time recover its force.

In the talk I had with him, Archimandrite Paul, placing the problem in the context of the present world situation, said:

«As a result of the steady disappearance of morality and religion, the world has reached the brink of the abyss. Having confronted the abyss, it is natural that it will recoil and return to objective moral and spiritual principles.»

AVVAKUM AND HIS HERMITAGE

From Karakallou I proceeded to the Monastery of Lavra, a journey that was by no means easy. It is a four hour walk on a stone-paved mule path in very poor condition, repeatedly ascending to the mountains and descending to the shore. Anyone making this trip in warm weather becomes very thirsty. Fortunately, there are occasional creeks with excellent cold water. The scenery is fascinating, particularly the sight of Athos from various angles as it rises to its awe-inspiring marble peak above the green mountain tops. Lavra remained invisible until I was just a few minutes away from it.

I remembered vividly the talks I had with Father Avvakum during my previous visit to Lavra and was on the lookout for him when I arrived. I saw him early in the morning, the day after my arrival, at the door of one of the side buildings of the refectory. He was about to leave for his hermitage *(esychastirion)*, and asked me if I would like to join him.

«You will like the place,» he said smiling. «It's so beautiful, it's an earthly paradise.»

«I shall be delighted to come,» I replied. «How long will we stay there?»

«We shall stay there until midafternoon. I'll have to be back here before the vesper service. It's two weeks since I last went there, and I must go and water a young fig tree that I planted recently in the vineyard and remove the weeds that must have grown all over the place.»

We left the monastery and took the road that leads to the Rumanian Skete of Prodromou. Avvakum was barefooted, wore a ragged cassock, and held a crude walking stick. Over his left shoulder he had slung a small sack made of goat's hair, containing some provisions, as we were to have lunch at the hermitage. Although he is sixty-five, Avvakum possesses a body which is physiologically that of a young man. Of medium stature, he is slim, upright, agile, and possesses astonishing endurance. Fatigue seems to be unknown to him. He walked rapidly, and talked or prayed all of the way. I let him lead the conversation. Throughout our journey, which took an hour and a half, he dwelt on God, saints, and religious themes in general. At frequent intervals, whenever he stopped talking, he uttered the Prayer of Jesus: «Lord Jesus Christ, Son of God, have mercy upon me.»

AVVAKUM

When we were some distance from Lavra, we heard a nightingale singing, and Avvakum said:

«Do you hear the little bird singing? It is glorifying God.»

This remark brought to my mind Psalm 150, which is sung by the Athonite monks every morning during the *orthros:* «Let every thing that has breath praise the Lord.»

Avvakum has complete trust in God. He has surrendered entirely to the Divine Will.

«Whatever you undertake to do,» he told me, «always invoke God and say, ‹Let this be done if it is good.›»

He narrated various incidents from the lives of saints showing their complete surrender to God's will, as well as their other virtues. After narrating each incident, he would ask me:

«Did you know that?»

If I answered with a «No,» he would urge me to read it in the Dukakis' *Great Collection of Lives of Saints.*

«Buy this work and read it,» advised Avvakum. «It is the great philosophy.»

Shortly before we reached his hermitage, Avvakum left the main road and went to visit an old hermit who lives permanently nearby.

«Wait here for a few minutes,» he said. «I am going to give a loaf of bread to the old man, and I'll be right back. He is a very good person. I keep my library of about a hundred books here for safety. A madman lives in this region, and he has broken into my hut a number of times and taken away some of my books. Eventually he brought them back, but in bad condition.»

When Avvakum returned, we proceeded to his hermitage. This is located ten minutes below the Skete of Prodromou, in a region known as Vigla, «observation point,» so named because one enjoys from here a very extensive view of the sea below and of Mount Athos behind.

«Is it not as I told you? Is it not a little paradise?» asked Avvakum with a quiet smile.

«Yes, indeed,» I replied, as I viewed the beautiful vineyard and the scattered young fig and olive trees, and felt a refreshing breeze sweeping across the whole area.

«It's here,» said Avvakum, «that I have learned what I know—I mean the Holy Scriptures and the teachings of the Fathers. At one time I lived at this place continuously for ten years and studied a great deal. Now I come here only occasionally, and each time I am filled with peace. At the monastery, I am weighed down with cares and can study only in snatches. Moreover, when I study there things don't get impressed on my mind deeply, and I don't retain them, whereas what I study here I retain.»

After this talk, Avvakum unlocked the door of his very old, tiny house, and brought out some things. Then he went to a sheltered place which he uses as a kitchen and drew a bucket of water from a deep, well-like cistern. He poured some of this water into a glass and gave it to me together with two pieces of loukoum. Avvakum's hermitage has no fountain or well. What little water he uses for drinking, cooking, watering young trees, and for other purposes, he draws up from the cistern. The water accumulates here during the rainy season from the tiled roof of the hut, being conducted to the cistern from the front edge of the roof by improvised gutters.

Having served me the sweet, Avvakum lit a fire, using dry twigs, and prepared some coffee for us. Before sipping his cup, he put some embers in a clay censer and censed the house and the newly constructed chapel, which is about fifty yards away.

For hours after this Avvakum was busy pulling weeds from the vineyard and tying up loose branches of the vines. He worked with real zest during the entire period, being particularly filled with joy as he saw that the trees and vines he had planted were thriving and bearing abundant fruit, and that the new building was nearing completion. This building will include a chapel, rooms for Avvakum and one or two other monks, and a guestroom. All the money that he has been receiving for years from the Monastery of Lavra as his regular allotment has been going towards the purchase of materials and the payment of labor for the construction. Also, the money he has been getting from selling the grapes of the vineyard — whatever grapes are left after he has given away to monks and others who visit him here — he has been spending for the same purpose. Avvakum intends to retire here when he becomes really old and unable to work at the monastery. In the meantime, the building will be needed for his occasional retreats, as the old hut is about ready to collapse.

Around noon, Avvakum returned to the hut, lit a new fire, sliced some squash, and began frying it for lunch. When the squash was ready, he put it on two plates which he set on a table in front of the hut. Then he took a loaf of dark bread from his bag, a few scallions, a piece of cheese, and a small bottle of wine and set them on the table. Lunch being ready, Avvakum invited me to eat.

Our meal started and ended with a prayer. While we were eating, the monk spoke about various religious subjects. At one point I interjected this question:

«Father Avvakum, you have said so much today about sacred matters and saints. Tell me, is it possible for one who lives in the world to attain sainthood?»

«It is very difficult,» he replied, «but not impossible. St. John Chrysostom says that ‹It is not the place *(topos)*, but the way of life *(tropos)* that makes saints.› However, he exhorts men who live in the world to go to the fathers of the desert and confess to them.

In other words, according to Avvakum, spiritual development of a very high order, denoted by the term sainthood, *can* be achieved by one who lives in the world; but this is very difficult and requires oral instruction and guidance by a holy man who lives in seclusion. The place where one lives, whether the wilderness or the world, is not the sole or even the main factor in the process of one's inner evolution; nevertheless it does play an important role: seclusion is conducive to it, whereas life in the world hinders it.

RUMANIAN SKETE OF PRODROMOU

Shortly after our meal, we left the hermitage and headed for the coenobitic Rumanian Skete of Prodromou, «the Forerunner,» which is a dependency of the Monastery of Lavra that acquired the status of a skete in 1852, having been a *kelli* up to that time. Avvakum stayed here only a few minutes, as he had to return to Lavra quickly to get ready for a special vesper service that was to be held in the Chapel of St. Michael Synadon, in honor of this saint. He had to wash up, put on his new cassock, and prepare the refreshments that were to be given to the congregation at the end of the service. Before leaving, he took from his sack the bread that was left over from our meal and gave it to one of the monks whom he knew by name. The monk accepted it with many thanks.

This monk, named Clement, and some others I met, knew very little Greek, and it was impossible for me to carry on much of a conversation with them. Among the bits of information I gathered from them was that the skete now has twenty-two monks, but formerly had over eighty; and that it is in great poverty because Rumania has deprived it of the estates it had there and doesn't send it any financial aid.

Walking about in the courtyard, I could see that this skete, which looks like an Athonite monastery, consisting of a quadrangle of buildings and a centrally located main church, is indeed in a rather unfortunate state. Poverty is visible everywhere. The monks are dressed in ragged clothes and even in sacks. The buildings, including the main church, which is a large domed structure, are disintegrating, as the monks have neither the time nor the financial resources for their proper upkeep. These poor but industrious and devout monks have to struggle for physical survival, cultivating their vegetable gardens about the skete, fishing, and occasionally working for the nearby monastic establishments.

In spite of its great poverty, the Skete of Prodromou retains a good deal of its original beauty and dignity, enhanced by two rows of tall, graceful cypresses on the north and south side of the courtyard.

SKETE OF KAPSOKALYVIA

I returned to Lavra, and after three days I went to another dependency of this monastery, the Greek Skete of Kapsokalyvia, two hours away by foot. This skete, which is idiorrhythmic and looks like a village with widely scattered houses, was founded in the eighteenth century. It is built on an abrupt slope of the Mountain, and its buildings, especially the main church and the houses near it, present an extremely beautiful and spectacular sight as one approaches it from the road that goes there from Lavra. Altogether there are about forty *kalyves,* inhabited by sixty to seventy monks.

When I arrived, there was not a soul in sight. So I went to the principal church and pulled the rope that was attached to one of the bells in the bell tower, ringing it three or four times. This is the customary way of summoning the *dikaios,* or prior, when he is not in or near the guesthouse. After several minutes, a robust young monk arrived. He was the *dikaios.* I should explain that the *dikaios* is elected annually by the elders of the skete, lives in a house separately set aside for him, near the guesthouse, and provides hospitality to visitors. His house is near the *kyriakon,* the community's principal church.

This *dikaios,* named Luke, invited me into the guesthouse, and prepared some food for me. During the meal and later on I talked with him about the skete and also about iconography, as he is a painter of icons. Regarding the skete, he explained that according to tradition it derives its name from a fourteenth century saint named Maximos Kapsokalyvitis, who lived a hermit's life in this region. This Maximos practiced interior prayer (*noera prosefhi*) and is credited with extraordinary religious experiences. Both for the sake of cultivating extreme non-attachment to material things and for developing great humility by pretending to be a fool, he did not settle down in one place, but moved about, building a hut out of straw and setting it afire after a time, then making another one, which after a while he would similarly set on fire. His practice of thus destroying his huts led to his being named *Kapsokalyvitis,* «the man who sets huts on fire.»

I had occasion to meet Luke's elder (*gerontas*), a priest-monk named Eugene. Although he had heart-trouble and was planning to go to Thessaloniki for medical treatment, Eugene did not dwell on his health, but spoke about iconography and monasticism. He himself is an iconographer, and like the rest of the iconographers at Kapsokalyvia he now paints both in the Byzantine and in the modern style. I asked Eugene if there was much demand for icons made on Athos.

«The demand,» he replied, «is small. The money we get barely suffices for our necessities. Before Russia became communist, there was such a demand for Athonite icons that the icon painters of the Mountain were all kept busy and still couldn't meet it. The Russians used to take whole shiploads of icons to their country. That's all over. Now we have to wait for an occasional order from the Greeks.»

Father Eugene's statements about Russia made me wonder whether the tremendous Russian demand for icons from Athos was not the main factor that led to the gradual abandonment of the Byzantine tradition of iconography on the Mountain in the last century. For beginning with the seventeenth century the Russians became increasingly modernistic in their iconography and presumably demanded from the monks of Athos icons done in the modern, secularized, Russo-Italian style.

When our conversation turned to monastic life, I asked Eugene how he found it.

«Monastic life,» he replied, «is beautiful, quiet, and of course good for the soul. I left Smyrna at the age of sixteen, of my own choice, and became a monk here. I have been on the Holy Mountain for fifty-six years and don't regret my choice in the least.»

With a middle-aged monk named Mark I talked about worship at Kapsokalyvia. Mark is a woodcarver; he makes wooden spoons, forks, combs, letter-openers, and other articles. Worship at this skete, he informed me, is similar to that at the monasteries, except that there is a liturgy only on Sundays and major holy days. The *orthros,* the vespers, and the *apodeipnon* are held in the chapels inside the various *kalyves*, while the liturgy and the vigils are held in the main church, and are attended by all the monks of the skete.

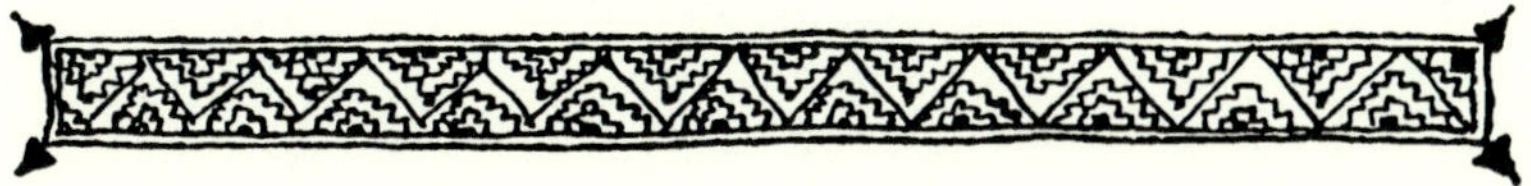

HERMITS AT KAROULIA

Continuing my journey southwestward, I went to the hermitages of Karoulia, which are a quarter of an hour's walk from the house of the Danielaioi at Katounakia.

KAROULIA

These hermitages are in the most secluded and inaccessible region of the Holy Mountain. The huts of the hermits are built on very abrupt rocks or on rather steep terraced cliffs, near the sea, at the south end of the Athos peninsula. It was in this area that in 492 B.C. the mighty fleet of the Persian commander-in-chief Mardonius was sunk by the furious sea.

There are nearly a score of hermits here, about half of whom are Greeks and the others Russians. I visited all the Greeks and most of the Russians. It was impossible to carry on a conversation with any of the Russians, except one who could speak English. The others knew only Russian and a few Greek words.

The first hermit I met was Father Gabriel, a Greek. When I came to the door of the enclosure of his hut, I pulled a cord that was evidently connected with a bell inside, and waited. After a while, a monk of about forty-five years of age, who looked like St. John the Baptist as depicted in Byzantine icons, opened the door. He asked me what I wanted, and having received my reply, let me in.

This hut consists of a closet-sized chapel and three tiny rooms built in a cave. Below it there is a frightening abyss, while above it there is a rocky cliff that rises at an almost ninety degree angle.

Gabriel asked me to sit down. I sat on a small bench and started asking him the usual questions: where he came from, how long he had been on Athos, how he found life here. I learned that he was an Athenian and that he had lived in this hut for twenty years, sharing it until just a few years ago with his spiritual father. Since the latter's death he has lived here all alone. Our conversation turned quickly to the spiritual life. Gabriel spoke as follows:

«There are a number of important things that should be observed by those seeking spiritual development. One of these is physical and mental quiet *(esychia)*, made possible by living in a quiet place, away from noise, confusion, and distractions.

«Control of talking is another. Such control helps bring about inner silence, which strengthens a person spiritually, whereas unnecessary talking does the reverse.

«Fasting is indispensable. It purifies the body, disciplines the soul, and helps the mind exercise inner attention.

«Inner attention, observing vigilantly one's thoughts and emotions, and opposing those that are bad or useless, is quite essential. Without it, prayer cannot be effective.

«Mental prayer is most important, and should be practiced constantly. This form of prayer consists in invoking mentally the name of Christ, saying: ‹Lord Jesus Christ, Son of God, have mercy upon me.› During such prayer one should strive to bring the mind into the heart, to unite thought with feeling.»

I asked Father Gabriel whether he recommended the *Philokalia* for persons who, while living in «the world, were interested in these practices and wanted to become familiar with them and to make proper use of them. He gave the following reply:

«The *Philokalia* is an excellent work, but it is for those who are advanced in the life of spiritual striving. It is ‹university› education. First one has to go to ‹grammar school,› then to ‹high school,› and only then is he ready to go to a‹university›»

«Should one start with *Evergetinos?*»

«No,» he replied. «This, too, is advanced: it's ‹high school.› One must start with something more elementary. One should read the lives of saints *(synaxaria)*, in order to learn what kind of men the saints were, how they lived, and what they did. Then one can proceed to the higher steps.»

«It is necessary,» he continued, «that one have a spiritual guide. Without such a person nothing can be achieved. Take an art or trade: in order to learn it properly, one has to become an apprentice to a master artist or tradesman. This is even more true in the case of the spiritual life, which is ‹the art of arts and the science of sciences,› as the Fathers say.

Gabriel spoke with deep conviction and feeling, in a kind yet austere manner.

When I was about to leave, he went and brought me a handful of almonds. I refused to take them, realizing that these constituted one of the few articles of food that the hermit had in this wilderness. But he insisted that I take them, and I yielded. I have seldom been so deeply touched by a person's hospitality. This act of Father Gabriel reminded me of the poor widow of whom Christ speaks, who cast two mites into the treasury, «out of her poverty putting in all the living that she had» (Mark 12: 42-44).

When I left Father Gabriel, I resumed my walk down the narrow, zigzag, cobbled path that starts some distance from the house of the Danielaioi and goes all the way down to the beach, terminating at a stone pier. Both the path and the pier were constructed not long ago by the Danielaioi to facilitate the transportation of their icons to the boats and also of provisions from the boats to their house. Mules can go up and down this rather steep track. The region through which it passes is not so abrupt and rocky as the rest of Karoulia. There are a few terraces with almond, fig, and olive trees. Most of the soil of the terraces has been brought from other places. Here and there one comes across big prickly pear cactuses, the only plants that thrive at Karoulia. The others remain small and weak and bear little fruit.

Soon after I arrived at the beach I met an elderly hermit, dressed in ragged clothes. He had come to gather a certain variety of shellfish for making rosaries *(kombologia)*. Upon learning that I was from America, he asked me about the present spiritual state of the Americans. He showed no interest whatever in political or economic matters. As he had not yet gathered enough shellfish, he begged me to excuse him, so that he might continue his search, and invited me to visit him after about an hour at his little dwelling, which he pointed out to me.

Presently, another hermit, who had come to the shore for the same purpose, came and greeted me. He was considerably younger than the other, probably in his late forties. A conversation started, and the monk invited me to his hut to have coffee and to continue our talk away from the hot sun. I accepted his invitation and followed him up a very steep path to his hut, which is continuous with a cave bigger than the hut itself.

«Why did I come here? you will ask me,» said the hermit, whose name was John. «*For the sake of eternity.* Our life here on earth, whether we are plain folks, scientists or professors, princes or kings, will inevitably come to an end. When we die, these titles and capacities will mean nothing, absolutely nothing. The only thing that will matter then will be the quality of our soul, whether it is good or bad, whether we have saved it or lost it. Heaven and hell are everlasting, whereas our earthly life is insignificantly brief.»

«I was born in Athens, where I had a good job in a department store,» John went on, «and could in time have become the owner of such a store. But I gave it up. I left Athens eighteen years ago, renouncing mother, father, friends and my way of life, and came to Athos.»

John paused for a few moments, and then added, smiling:

«At one time, when I was in ‹the world,› I dreamed of going to America and becoming an actor in Hollywood, as I felt that I had all that was needed to be a success in such a profession.»

In connection with this «dream» of John, I should explain that it was not based on a false estimate of himself. John is tall, handsome, with a classical Greek profile, blue eyes and blond hair, and is gifted in speech. It's likely that he had been urged to become an actor.

«I sought happiness,» he went on, «the way people usually seek it—in backgammon, dances, picnics, and the like. But every time I engaged in these I returned home disappointed. I felt more and more the vanity of such things. In religion, on the other hand, I found something really satisfying. My decision finally to become a monk resulted from visits to a church that followed the old calendar. I was deeply moved by the contrition and piety of the congregation, and became seriously interested in Orthodoxy, and finally resolved to live it in its highest, most austere form.»

For John, Orthodoxy is the supreme, most important thing in life, in comparison with which everything else sinks into insignificance. But this Orthodoxy must be faithful to Tradition in all respects. John is one of those monks who are known as «zealots,» because of their severely ascetic way of life and their great strictness in all matters pertaining to Orthodoxy.

With what does John occupy himself? He prays, reads religious works, and makes rosaries. In the tiny room in which we sat, I saw a copy of the *Philokalia,* some other works by Nicodemos, and the *Ascetic Discourses* of St. Isaac the Syrian. During our talk he took up one of these books and read something in it that referred to prayer; he recommended to me the practice of the Prayer of Jesus.

ROSARY

John earns the small amount of money that he needs for his bare necessities by making rosaries with the shells of shellfishes or with woolen threads. The woolen rosaries are of different sizes and colors: some are black, others blue, etc. They all have a hundred knots, each one of them made carefully by a very skilful manipulation of the threads, so as to form, according to John, seven crosses. The other hermits at Karoulia earn their living the same way, or by making baskets and brooms.

«What about water in this desert?» I asked John.

«This,» he replied, «is provided by well-like cisterns that accumulate water during the rainy seasons. Some of them are made of cement, while others consist of hollows made in the rock. Water has to be used very sparingly, because there is so little of it. When one of us runs short of water, the others gladly supply him from theirs.»

«It is probably very cold here in the winter,» I remarked.

«Sometimes it is, but most of the time it's not,» John said. «Our winters are among the mildest on Athos. Karoulia is out of the way of the north wind, and the sun shines on us from early morning until sunset.»

After he had offered me some coffee and water, and knit a rosary in order to show me how it is made, my host volunteered to act as my guide to the little houses on the abrupt rocks below the hut of Father Gabriel. Very few people have visited these huts, because the region where they are built is terrifying to look at. No amount of coaxing, even by a spirited hermit like John, will induce most persons who come this way—and these are few—to attempt to climb over this area. We walked to a spot below Gabriel's hut and then began to descend the vertical rock. John led the way. He warned me not to look behind me at the sea below, because this might make me dizzy and cause me to lose my hold. We descended slowly, holding firmly onto a chain with both hands and stepping into small grooves that hardly provided space for our toes. After a while we reached a spot where the rock projects somewhat. We stopped here for a few minutes, and John showed me an enormous cave under the rock. The

KAROULIA

hermits, he told me, use this cave as a workshop for making baskets and brooms. Another chain connects this place with the region below. Further down, in addition to a chain, there are two wooden ladders. The chains and the ladders are fastened onto the rocks by means of nails, some of which appear almost entirely gone from rust. Having gone down these ladders, we reached the lowest inhabited spot. Here there is a two-storied hut with a wooden balcony that extends over the sea. From the balcony hangs a rope from a pulley which is attached to a pole. The Greek word for pulley is *karouli,* and it is the use of such *karoulia* that has given the region its name. Two Greek monks live in this house, but they were absent at the time of our visit. John explained that they tie a basket to one end of the rope and lower it down to draw up supplies from the boats. They also leave it lowered at times, hoping that some fisherman will put a piece of bread in it.

Having seen the little house, we started climbing the rock, taking a different route from the one we took to descend. The mountainside was not quite as sheer as in the previous route, though here, too, we had to use chains and ropes. When we reached the road that connects the pier of Karoulia with the house of the Danielaioi, we parted. John's last words to me were these:

«Work for your earthly country, America, but even more for the Heavenly Country of us all. And your reward shall be great in Heaven.»

John walked downhill in the direction of his hut, while I went to the house of the Danielaioi to eat and stay overnight. Early the next morning, I climbed down the rather precipitous cliff I had ascended with John the day before. I stopped at the first hut I came to, knocked on the door, and waited. I heard movements inside. Then the door opened and I saw before me a tall, very slim, upright, elderly hermit with a large white beard, wrinkled face, and clear, bright eyes. He was barefooted and wore ragged clothes and an old monastic cap.

«What do you want, my son?» he asked serenely.

«I would like to talk with you, to learn about your life here, and benefit from your experience,» I replied.

«I am sorry, but I am a simple and illiterate man. What will you learn from me? But come in, and we'll talk. Or let us sit out here, if you prefer.»

«It's windy, and I am perspiring,» I said. «It would be better if we went inside.»

The hut of this hermit, whose name is Philaretos, consists of two extremely small rooms, separated by a partition. The room into which he invited me was about six foot square and had a single window on the side that faced the sea. The floor was wooden and bare. The only furniture in the room was a wooden box. The hermit asked me to sit on it, while he himself sat on the floor and leaned against the wall. He began to talk.

«I came to the Holy Mountain when I was seventeen. I am now seventy years old. The greater part of my stay on the Mountain has been at the Monastery of Stavronikita. I have been here at Karoulia during the last ten years. At the age of seventeen, I planned to go to America, and had actually made preparations. But something unexpected happened that upset my plans, and I came to the Holy Mountain instead. It was the Grace of the *all-good* God that brought me here.»

Philaretos uttered the words «*all-good* God» with a deep feeling of gratitude and contrition, crossing himself.

Besides profound reverence for God, Philaretos showed a humility that knows no bounds:

«I am the worst man,» he said. «I am worse than rubbish.»

Why did he come to this terrifying wilderness?

«We have renounced everything and have come here,» he said, «from our love for God and for the salvation of our soul. A man should strive to save his soul. If one fails in this, everything one has done has been in vain. Many people cannot understand why we insist so much on certain things, which for them are details not worth bothering about. But we who have come here cannot look that way at matters pertaining to our religion. *We watch every little detail, lest we fail in our purpose.*»

In referring to people who cannot understand the importance assigned by him and other monks, known as «zealots,» to little details, Philaretos did not manifest even a trace of spite or indignation.

The practice that Philaretos stressed most of all was mental prayer.

«Repeat the Prayer of Jesus as much as you can,» he advised, «saying mentally in your heart: ‹Lord Jesus Christ, Son of God, have mercy upon me.› This is best done sitting quietly in your room.»

Regarding his diet, Philaretos said:

«I eat very sparingly. When I work for others, as for instance in road repairing or construction, I eat nothing until I return to my hut. I avoid artificial and canned foods. They are not good for one's health. You probably know that we hermits seldom eat cooked food. Our diet consists mainly of dry bread or zwieback, olives, soaked faba beans, and leafy vegetables.»

I asked Philaretos how he warmed his hut in cold weather. He replied:

«A man should not keep an even temperature where he lives. He should accustom himself to the changes of temperature throughout the year. I never light a fire in my house, even for cooking. Whenever I want to cook anything, I light a fire outside. I keep warm in the winter by putting on more clothes, eating a little more food, performing more prostrations, and occasionally when it is sunny or fair sitting outside in a sheltered spot absorbing warmth from the sun.»

«Does anyone come and help you in any way?»

«No one. I sew and mend my clothes, repair my shoes and hut, prepare my food, and do everything else myself.»

In spite of his very austere mode of life, Philaretos enjoys excellent health and is quite happy.

«I never go to a doctor or take medicines,» he told me. «I have found that the best medicine is complete fasting, that is, abstaining from all food for a day or more and then eating fruits of the season. Glory to God! I enjoy good health and have everything I need to be happy.»

At this point he got up and asked me to follow him outside. He showed me the magnificent and awe-inspiring contours of the rock, the scattered shrubs that are wedged in it, a few wild flowers, his tiny vegetable garden and a vine in the proximity of his house, and the deep blue sea below. These things, which Philaretos sees not merely as aesthetic objects, but as manifestations of God's power and goodness, are a source of gladness to him.

«Look,» he said, pointing at a potato plant in his

garden. «You take a potato and bury it in the soil and out of it grows a plant with beautiful leaves and flowers, and a cluster of other potatoes. How marvellous! And if the *all-good* God [Philaretos crossed himself] produces such wonderful things here, how much greater marvels await those who shall enter Heaven. O! How good God is, and how grateful we ought to feel towards Him!»

After about an hour's stay at Philaretos', I asked him if he would do me the favor of taking me to the Russian priest-monk Nikon, who I knew lived in this area. Philaretos expressed his willingness, but begged me to wait a little, in order that he might bring me a treat before leaving his house. He brought me a biscuit made of whole wheat flour, sweetened with honey, and a little can full of water. In offering these to me he apologized for not having anything better. I accepted his treat with sincerely felt thanks.

Shortly after, Philaretos took me to Nikon's house, only a few yards away. He knocked on the door of the enclosure and we waited. When the door opened, Philaretos introduced me to his neighbor as best he could—Nikon speaks little Greek. The monk welcomed me inside. Before leaving us, the Greek hermit asked me to return to his hut when I was through, so that he might take me to other monks of Karoulia.

The Russian hermit led me to his house, which is larger than Philaretos', and has a chapel inside, and asked me to sit on a bench that was outside along the wall. He sat down beside me. We conversed in English, which he speaks fluently, with a British intonation.

Nikon had been a higher officer in Tzarist Russia. He left Russia during the Bolshevik upheaval and lived subsequently in various European countries, especially England, until about 1935, when he withdrew to Mount Athos. I have been told that he corresponds with certain distinguished Europeans and Americans, some of whom occasionally come to Athos to see him. He has written the Foreword to *Writings from the Philokalia on Prayer of the Heart.*

«I feel very low,» said Nikon, when I asked him about his health. «I have been feeling so for months now. My eyesight, hearing, and memory have been failing. Also my heart has been causing me trouble.»

He spoke haltingly. There were frequent intervals of silence, as I waited for him to resume the conversation. Although eighty-five and in failing health, he showed surprising vigor of intellect and of will. He spoke in a brusk manner, and expressed himself with conciseness and emphasis.

The previous day, a German mechanical engineer from the Latin American countries had visited Nikon.

«Did you by any chance meet him?» Nikon asked.

«Yes,» I replied. «I met him last night at the house of the Danielaioi, where he came to pass the night after he had left you.»

«What did you think of him?»

«He seemed to be very much interested in religion. He told me that he had visited India and had studied Buddhism and other religions there. When I and one of the monks asked him why he had come to the Holy Mountain, he answered that he had come here to become acquainted with Orthodox monasticism. And when he was asked what he thought of Athonite monasticism, now that he had the opportunity of studying it, he replied that he found it extremely interesting and that he believed it led to the *same* goal as the religions he had studied in India, but led to that goal *faster.* He added that as a consequence he was thinking seriously of becoming an Orthodox monk.»

«He told me that, too,» said Nikon. «But how can one

understand Orthodox monasticism without having any Orthodox blood, without having Orthodox roots? In the present overwhelmingly materialistic age, even peoples that have been Orthodox for many centuries can hardly understand Orthodoxy.»

Our conversation turned to the English version of the *Philokalia.*

«I had the stupidity,» said the hermit, «to write the Foreword to the volume that was published in 1951. But [he chuckled] I didn't sign my name. People today cannot understand such writings. The interest shown in them is mainly due to their novelty, to the fact that they are something unknown and different. It doesn't spring from a real understanding and appreciation. Eastern Orthodoxy is Christianity's *maximum,* it is *the only the truth.* To understand it, one must have a certain degree of inner development. But men's spiritual level today is extremely low.»

I didn't have to ask how Father Nikon liked Karoulia. Twice during our conversation he paused, looked around, and remarked:

«This is a *splendid* place!»

As I was about to leave, I said to him:

«Is there anything you would like me to send you from Athens or America? It will be a great pleasure for me to send you something.»

«Thank you very much,» he remarked. «I don't need anything. The only thing I would care for would be a book on radio astronomy.»

«I shall send you one,» I said, and rose to depart.

Nikon accompanied me to the door of the enclosure, unlocked it, and let me out. He followed me for a few steps, and when I bid him goodby, he said:

«God bless you! Thanks for coming!»

I returned to Philaretos' hut as I had promised. He was ready to take me to some of the other hermits. Leaving his house, we went to Bartholomew, who is somewhat younger than Philaretos. We found him sitting in front of his hut weaving a basket. Bartholomew came to Athos at the end of the First World War, after serving in the Greek army for five years. I asked him what made him decide to come to the Mountain and become a monk.

«It was a call from God, it was God's Grace,» he replied.

Although he lives in very great poverty, almost as extreme as Philaretos', Bartholomew would not let me go without having something. He offered me a little cup of coffee, a piece of loukoum, and a glass of water.

Next we visited Dionysios. He happened to be inside his hut, and welcomed us in. I begged him not to serve me any refreshments, saying that I just had some, but my words did not prevail on him.

The last hermit we visited at Karoulia was the priest-monk Pachomios. He lives in the last hut I visited the previous day, the one with the balcony and the pulley. Pachomios invited us inside and showed us a basket he had been making. Then he took us out to the balcony, and afterwards to the chapel. The latter is surprisingly large, considering the size of the house and the abrupt place on which it is built. One marvels at the faith and skill of the hermits that built these structures, as well as at the hardiness of the present dweller. It is a feat just to descend to this house; to dwell in it the year round, especially when the violent sea is pounding below and the powerful south wind is blowing on the sides, would try the endurance of all but few men.

When we were about to leave, Pachomios went into one of the rooms and brought a few pieces of cheese, an onion, and two handfuls of odd ends and bits of dark bread which he had probably received from one of the monasteries, wrapped them in a cloth napkin and gave them to

Philaretos. At first Philaretos refused to take them, saying that he still had some food at home. But Pachomios finally persuaded him to take them, by telling him that he might pass them on to someone else.

Upon leaving Pachomios, we climbed up the sheer rock that rises above Pachomios' house, passing the large cave I had seen the day before. When we reached the other side of Karoulia, we took a steep narrow path that goes through Katounakia, and stopped on our way at several of the hermitages and talked with the inhabitants.

Late in the afternoon, Philaretos and I parted. I felt very much obliged to him. Before bidding him good-by, I asked him what he would like me to send him when I returned to «the world.»

«Nothing,» he replied categorically. «I have every good, and am happier than a king. You would cause me grief if you send me anything whatsoever.»

Thus ended a day's association with a man who, although he is old in years, is young in body; although he considers himself «the worst of men,» is really a saint; and although he has nothing, yet possesses all things (2 Cor. 6 : 10).

About Philaretos I was later to learn the following incident from Father Theodosios of the Monastery of St. Paul, editor of the periodical *St. Paul of Xeropotamou.* Months before we met, Philaretos had been summoned to appear in court at Thessaloniki. The reason for this was that someone who had visited the Holy Mountain went to Karoulia and broke into a hermit's house and stole some articles. As he was not caught, several persons, including Philaretos, were called to testify. With the strictness that characterizes him in all matters, Philaretos refused to swear that he spoke the truth, asserting that taking an oath is contrary to Christ's injunction which says: «Do not swear at all,... but let what you say be simply ‹Yes› or ‹No;› anything more than this comes from evil» (Matt. 5: 34, 37). Philaretos' refusal to take an oath led to his imprisonment for a period of four months, as the penal law of Greece states that anyone who refuses to testify under oath should be punished. This was his first contact with «the world» after a period of more than fifty years on Mount Athos. What is remarkable about the incident is that Philaretos endured his imprisonment without getting at all upset, but retaining his customary calm throughout. He considered his sentence a chastisement inflicted upon him by God Himself for some element of vainglory that must have been lurking in him.

THE TWO ST. ANNES

Leaving Karoulia, I headed northwestward for the Skete of St. Anne, accompanied by a young deacon of the Danielaioi, Father Gregory, who was going there for some matter. On the way, we passed through a group of *kalyves* known as Little St. Anne, only a short distance from Katounakia. This settlement, which is appended to the Skete of St. Anne, is connected with two prominent monks, one of them past and the other contemporary. The older monk is Agapios Landos (17th cent.), author of *The Salvation of Sinners, The New Paradise,* and other books, while the present one is the hymnographer Gerasimos.

Father Gregory explained that Gerasimos is an extremely gifted writer of hymns. He is unique not only on the Holy Mountain, but in all of Greece. Gerasimos is about fifty-five years of age and has been on Athos since 1923. So far he has composed about a hundred fifty full church services and has made additions to about eighty others. Further, he has written over a hundred supplicatory canons, more than two hundred troparia to various saints, and numerous other compositions. The language and style in which he writes are those of the great Byzantine hymnographers.

The following brief hymns from his book *Apolytikia, Kontakia, and Megalynaria* (Athens, 1957) will give some idea about the character of his poetry:

MEGALYNARION ON THE NATIVITY OF CHRIST

«Let every creature that has breath cry out joyfully,

Glory in the highest to the Savior Who was born in Bethlehem. For He has been seen on the earth bestowing peace; let us venerate the Divine Birth» (p. 69).

MEGALYNARION ON THE TRANSFIGURATION OF CHRIST

«Wishing to exhibit to Thy disciples power from Above and Wisdom from the Father, Thou went up Mount Tabor, O Christ, and having shone as the Master, Thou illuminated them» (p. 184).

APOLYTIKION TO THE APOSTLES PETER AND PAUL

«Peter and Paul, divine heralds, twin-fount of godliness, revealers of divine knowledge and heavenly doctrines, you have clearly distinguished yourselves as Supreme among the divine Apostles; now request for us the illumination that leads to salvation, deliverance from passions, and God's great mercy» (p. 161).

Father Gerasimos was not at Little St. Anne when we passed by. He had gone to Athens for the publication of some of his works.

The Skete of St. Anne, where I stayed for the night and a major part of the next day, is a dependency of the Monastery of Lavra. It is the oldest and largest idiorrhythmic skete on the Holy Mountain, having been organized into a community in 1666 and comprising fifty-eight houses, inhabited by a hundred and ten monks. Most of the monks are woodcavers or icon painters. I had the opportunity of talking with the *dikaios,* Father Panteleïmon, his assistant, Father Maximos, and a number of other monks, as well as of visiting several *kalyves.*

The presence of Maximos in the guesthouse, where there were about half a dozen guests, greatly enlivened it. Maximos is young and alert. He was eager to help the guests in every possible way, and at the table his contagious cheerfulness and wit made everyone eat with relish.

In the morning, I attended the liturgy in the cemetery chapel, which is near the main church. A liturgy is performed in this chapel every day. Through the windows I noticed that the basement was filled with human bones. Evidently the hermits here are not averse to such a sight, but seem to welcome it as a vivid reminder of death, serv-

SKETE OF ST. ANNE

ing to strengthen their resolve to despise everything trivial and vain, and to follow the «strait and narrow path.» St. John Climacos, whose *Ladder* is widely read on Athos, says in this book that «Just as bread is the most necessary of all foods, so the remembering of death is the most necessary of all practices» (Migne, *P.G.*, 88, 793). And Hesychios (died

ST. ANNE PRAYING

c. 433) says: «Let us remember death incessantly, if possible. Through memory of death are engendered in us the putting away of all cares and vanities, the guarding of the mind, ceaseless prayer, the freeing of the body from passions, and the loathing of sin. Indeed, if we are to tell the truth, almost every virtue springs from it» (*Philokalia,* I, 97).

After the liturgy, I visited a monk named John, whom an Athenian friend knew personally and had urged me to see. John lives with two other monks. All three of them are plain, humble, kindly men, but John, who is about seventy and is the elder of the house, is an especially sympathetic type of person. Like the other monks of the skete, they earn their living by the work of their hands, such as painting icons.

The house of these monks is crudely built of rubble that has been plastered over. On the side that faces the sea it has a wooden porch which overlooks a terraced garden. I was invited to have dinner with them on this porch. After dinner we all retired for a nap. I lay down on a divan in the central room of first floor, which serves as a guest room and living room, while the monks went to rest to their rooms upstairs. I might explain that the practice of an afternoon nap is observed elsewhere on Athos, too, and is necessitated by the long early morning church services and the frequent all-night vigils.

Although extremely poor, John would not let me go without accepting some humble gifts. He gave me two rosaries, one for myself and one for our Athenian friend, and a pocket-size *Tetraevangelion* containing the four Gospels and the Apocalypse. This work was published on Mount Athos in 1933 and is a faithful reprint of the Venice editions. John wrote orthographically the following dedication:

«I present this *Tetraevangelion* as a small gift and souvenir to Mr. C. The Monk John, icon painter, Kalyva of the Holy Forerunner *(Timios Prodromos)*, Skete of St. Anne, Holy Mountain.»

The name of the house is derived from its chapel, which is dedicated to St. John the Forerunner. Each house of the skete has its own chapel, in which services are held daily.

When I left these benevolent monks, I went to the

principal church of the skete, which is dedicated to St. Anne, mother of the Holy Virgin. This church is decorated with frescoes that were painted in 1757. Although not among the best on the Mountain, they show good craftsmanship, real understanding of the principles of true art, and genuine piety. In the center of the dome is depicted Christ as Pantocrator. In the circular strip immediately below is represented the «great entrance» of the liturgy, with Christ officiating, and a host of angels. Below this, between the windows of the dome-drum, are depicted the prophets; and further down, on the pendentives, the four gospel-writers. The background in all these paintings is blue.

Among the other wall paintings, I found the Nativity, which is painted on the east side of the south vault, adjacent to the apse of the south choir, especially interesting. The colors and forms are beautiful, the postures, gestures and facial expressions full of religious feeling. The swaddled babe in the manger is at the center of the composition. Above, at the upper part of the big dark opening of the cave, is a star. The heads of a cow and a horse, facing one another, are visible just behind the manger. In front, Joseph is kneeling to the left and Mary to the right of the manger in relation to the beholder. Approaching the entrance of the cave at the left are depicted the three Magi bearing gifts, while at the right side are an angel and a shepherd. In the sky above the cave are other angels, while in the foreground are depicted three shepherds, a dog, a flock of sheep, and a tree. One of the shepherds, a boy, is seated at the lower left hand corner, playing a pipe. In front of him is a dog, with its head turned around, looking at him. At the opposite corner, a young shepherd announces the Nativity, making a

gesture towards the cave with his right hand, to an old shepherd who is stooped and leans against his walking stick. White sheep are under and behind the tree at the middle of the foreground. The artist who painted this icon had little regard for natural proportions and perspective. Thus, the tree is rather small and schematic; the sheep are little and inconspicuous; the shepherds in the foreground are smaller instead of larger than Joseph and Mary, who are farther away, near the center of the composition; while the Babe is large compared to the figures in the foreground. It is clear that the artist has deliberately altered the natural proportions and reversed perspective, in order to emphasize what is more important and to play down what is less important.

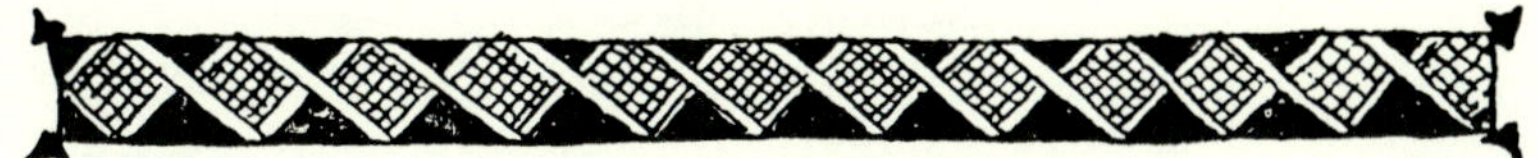

HERMITS OF NEW SKETE

From certain persons in Athens I had heard a great deal about two monks at New Skete, which lies near the sea northwest of the Skete of St. Anne. Now that I was only half an hour's walk away, I did not miss the opportunity of going there and meeting them.

New Skete is an idiorrythmic dependency of the Monastery of St. Paul that was founded in the eighteenth century. It has twenty-eight *kalyves* and fifty-five monks, most of whom are icon painters. The rest are tailors, shoemakers, sweatermakers, and woodcarvers, making mortars, receptacles and other artifacts by means of the lathe.

The two monks I went to see in particular were Joseph and Ephraim. Joseph is in his seventies, of short stature and medium build, with a good crop of grey hair and big, peaceful eyes. He is the spiritual father and guide of eight monks of this skete, and is regarded by them with great reverence.

When I met Joseph at his hut, which is about five minutes' walk from the *kyriakon,* the first thing we discussed was confession.

«Man,» said Father Joseph, «cannot escape God's eye, even as regards the smallest things, even in the most secret places; for God is present everywhere. He cannot lie to God, without God knowing that he is lying. So when a person confesses, he must tell the confessor the full truth about his deeds, thoughts, and feelings, hiding nothing. Such confession is essential for one's spiritual health and progress. It is a most important means of inner purification.»

Then Joseph asked me if I read the Gospels.

«It is good to read them *daily,*» he said. «Read also the Old Testament, especially certain parts of it, such as the Psalms. Dukakis' *Great Collection of Lives of Saints,* which has been re-edited recently by the monk Victor Matthew, is a very comprehensive work which I strongly recommend. The best time to read such writings is in the evening.»

«Don't neglect prayer,» he went on. «Practice especially mental prayer, or prayer of the heart, saying: ‹Lord Jesus Christ, Son of God, have mercy upon me.› This is the most important form of spiritual work.»

«But how can one practice this prayer in the world, where he is in the midst of so many cares and distractions?» I asked.

«Set aside an hour each day, preferably in the evening before going to bed, and practice it continuously during that time. I suggest also strongly that you read *The Way of a Pilgrim.* This book shows the importance of the prayer, and the manner in which it is to be practiced. The first part of this work is more valuable than the sequel *[i.e., The Pilgrim Continues His Way],* which seems to have been added by another author.»

«Some persons say that this prayer is hazardous for one's sanity,» I remarked.

«Of all forms of prayer,» said Joseph, «this is the safest and best, provided it is combined with inner attention, so that the mind does not wonder off, and that one follows the instructions of an experienced spiritual guide.»

«At first,» he continued, «this prayer should be said *orally.* Later, it should be said *mentally,* though even then it should be said orally when one cannot concentrate too well on it. As we practice this prayer, it becomes an inner activity that goes on unceasingly. And *it gives results*. You need not accept this assertion on trust. Your own experience will prove it. Experience proves the prayer of Jesus to be very effective as a means of purifying the heart and mind, of opening up the mind and revealing to it untold treasures.»

Joseph's reference to experience as a test of the value of mental prayer is quite in line, not only with the teachings of the great Byzantine mystics, but also with the modern demand for empirical verification. The recognition by the Byzantine mystics of an inner, experiential criterion is well illustrated by the following remarks of Nikephoros the Solitary and St. Gregory the Sinaite. «If you keep on praying in this manner,» says the first, speaking about the prayer of Jesus, «the way to the heart will be opened for you.... This is beyond doubt. We know from experience, that if you practice it with attention, the whole host of virtues will come to you: love, joy, peace, and so on» *(Philokalia,* 2, 241*)*. Similarly, St. Gregory the Sinaite (1255-1346), discussing how one may avoid being led astray in matters of good and evil, stresses the value of inner experience. «Do not allow yourself,» he says, «to be carried away by appearances, through light-mindedness, but remain weighty, and accept the good and reject the evil after careful testing; you ought to test and discriminate and only then believe» *(Philokalia,* 2, 278*)*.

Continuing his talk, Joseph said:

«Man's *chief* aim should be to *find God*. In finding God, he finds true happiness. The interior prayer we have been discussing leads man to Him. We can never thank God sufficiently for revealing Himself to us. We can never even thank Him enough for the other goods He bestows upon us. God need not have created man: He had hosts of angels. Yet He created man and countless marvellous things for him.»

During the entire conversation, Father Joseph spoke calmly and unaffectedly. He impressed me as being a genuine mystic, a true saint.

Joseph is not a mere contemplative. He is also a practical man, a teacher engaged in spiritually guiding, not only his entourage *(synodia)* at New Skete, but also other monks and laymen who seek instruction and counsel through visits and correspondence. All this he does *gratis,* from his intense love of God and neighbor.

Joseph recommended that I next visit Ephraim, who is a member of his *synodia.* This priest-monk lives in a little hut built on a cliff near the sea, a short distance from some caves that were formerly inhabited by hermits, but were abandoned in recent times when parts of the cliff above them began to break off.

Upon arriving at Ephraim's hut, I knocked on the door and waited. Presently I heard a gentle voice inside asking who it was. I answered, mentioning the fact that I had been sent by Father Joseph. The door was opened and I faced a handsome, delicately built monk, apparently in his twenties, with a full, black beard and very bright brown eyes. He invited me inside.

Ephraim explained that he lived here alone, but met Joseph and the other monks who were under Joseph's spiritual guidance twice a day: at church in the morning, where they had the liturgy, and at Joseph's house in the afternoon, for supper. The rest of the time, he said, he stayed in his own hut, practicing mental prayer and carving wooden crucifixes, little ones that are hung on the neck and larger ones that are employed by priests in church services. He handed me two beautiful crucifixes, one of each kind, to look at.

Regarding the place that mental prayer occupies for his group, Ephraim said that it was practiced every morning for six to seven hours continuously, and again in the

FATHER JOSEPH AND PART OF HIS GROUP

Joseph is at the center, seated; Ephraim, in priestly vestments, is at the extreme right

afternoon. In the morning, he explained, it took the place of the *orthros,* while in the afternoon it replaced the *apodeipnon.*

The things that Ephraim especially stressed in the conversation I had with him were: the monk's need of a spiritual guide, and the value of praying mentally and heeding one's conscience. As regards the first, he said:

«It is easy for one to become externally a monk, if he desires to, but to become one internally requires a whole science. This spiritual science has to be learned from an experienced possessor of it. Today, such men are rare. The spiritual decline of monasticism has resulted from the lack of men of this kind, who are called spiritual guides. To become a monk, one must first and foremost seek and find a spiritual guide. Everything depends upon this.»

«What,» I asked Father Ephraim, «is the chief feature of the guidance that a spiritual guide should provide to a monk?»

«It should be guidance concerning mental prayer. This mode of prayer is the *essence* of monasticism, its salt, its light, its life, and its glory. Yet it is precisely in this that the contemporary monk is very much in need of guidance. He hears about mental prayer, but he does not know how to practice it. And if he undertakes to proceed in this work relying on writings, he has the power to persist in it for a limited time only, because he encounters inner (*noeras*) difficulties on the way. Not having an experienced guide, he turns back convinced that he has need of one, without whom it is impossible to succeed.»

«What, specifically, are some of the fruits of mental prayer?» I asked.

«Mental prayer leads to deliverance from ‹passions.› The holy Fathers known as Vigilant (*Niptikoi*) teach us that only through the ceaseless practice of this prayer can this be achieved. ‹Out of the heart proceed evil thoughts, murders, adulteries, fornications, theft,› and so on, as the Gospel says [Matt. 15: 18]; but through the repeated invocation of Christ, the heart is purified of these. Having thus become pure, it turns into a source of divine illumination, spiritual love, joy, warmth, and peace. Man is regenerated, and becomes, as the holy Fathers say, *theophoros,* one who bears God within himself.»

Ephraim, as I have noted, also laid emphasis on heeding one's conscience.

«A peaceful conscience,» he said, «is one of the greatest sources of joy to man. Hence a person should listen attentively to it and always follow its promptings, so that it will denounce him in nothing.»

«But there is often a problem,» I remarked, «as to whether something is really prompted by our conscience and not by our subjective, fallible opinions or inclinations.»

«The solution to that,» said Ephraim, «is to seek to purify and enlighten conscience. Important means of achieving this are the reading of spiritual writings, especially the Gospels, and mental prayer.»

Ephraim's emphasis on the joy that a pure, peaceful conscience gives man reminded me of the following remarks that St. John Chrysostom makes in his second homily on St. Paul's Epistle to the Romans: «As for good spirits and joy, it is not greatness of power, not abundance of wealth, not pomp of authority, not strength of body, not sumptuousness of the table, not the adorning of dresses, nor any other of the things in man's reach that ordinarily produces them, but spiritual success and a good conscience alone. And he that has his conscience cleansed, even though he be clad in rags and struggling with famine, is of better spirits than they that live softly.» His indication of mental prayer as a means of purifying conscience is in accordance with the statement of St. John of Carpathos (7th cent.?) that «By our invoking of the name of our Lord Jesus Christ, our conscience is easily cleansed» (*Philokalia,* 1, 180).

END OF THE SOJOURN

After leaving New Skete, I visited the monasteries of St. Paul, Dionysiou, Grigoriou, Simonopetra, and finally Xeropotamou. At Dionysiou I found Father Theocletos busy writing the last pages of a book on the life and works of Nicodemos the Aghiorite, who was canonized in 1955. St. Nicodemos spent his first two years on Athos, between the ages of twenty-six and twenty-eight, at Dionysiou; and this was a special reason why Theocletos was greatly interested in him. Theocletos read me parts of his manuscript to get my reaction. It impressed me as a work written by one who knows the subject very well and seeks to present the personality and teaching of a Father of the Eastern Church in an edifying manner. The author characterized Nicodemos as the greatest post-Byzantine figure in Orthodox theology. I jotted down a passage that seemed to me of fundamental importance for understanding Orthodox monasticism.

«The present book,» says Theocletos in the preface, «is the work of a monk. In the Eastern Church, the existence of the ‹scholar› monk is quite unknown. What distinguishes Eastern Monasticism is a lived spirituality so elevated, that the monk finds no justification, under the Ascetic and Mystical Theology that has been developed by the Fathers, except as a worker of virtue, as a contemplative soul called by God, giving to his brethren in Christ, because of his love for them, out of the abundance of his experience of the divine.... Hence, the cell of the monk is

ST. NICODEMOS THE AGHIORITE

not a room for scholarly research and writing, but a place for prayer, work, meditation and the tempering of the soul for special spiritual struggles, in an unworldly, solitary, quiet region.»

At Xeropotamou I had occasion to talk with another very pious middle-aged monk named Gregory, who is a native of Larissa and has been a monk on Athos for twenty-two years. Gregory asked me about my place of origin, my occupation, and my journey on the Holy Mountain. When I had answered these questions, I expressed my desire to hear his views on Athonite monasticism. Characteristic among the statements he made in reply were the following:

«What business do we have being here, in these wild mountains? We could have stayed in ‹the world› and earned our living the way countless other people do. But we came here and have stayed here, because we had some prodigious experience. If this were not so, if God had not illumined us, we would not have given up mother, father, brothers, sisters, relatives, friends, possessions, enjoyments; and we would not have stayed here long. People today talk very lightly about monasticism, not knowing or understanding its aims. In fact, men have no idea of their destiny, of the true meaning of their life on earth. If they had, they would weep all day long for living so foolishly, so unbecomingly. God has bestowed great honor upon human nature, yet men live as if they were but beasts.»

When I was about to leave for Daphne, to return to Thessaloniki, I went to bid Gregory farewell. He greeted me very kindly and gave me these words of counsel:

«Take care of your soul. Do everything you possibly can for it. That is your most important task. The Apostle Paul says: ‹We look not at the things which are seen, but at the things which are not seen: for the things which are seen are temporal; but the things which are not seen are eternal›» (2 Cor. 4: 18).

CONCLUDING REMARKS

A journey to the Holy Mountain is a journey to Byzantium, to the great mediaeval Christian empire of the East. To have lived on the Holy Mountain is to have lived in that God-centered world. Except for the use of the motorboat to travel from some of the monasteries and monastic dependencies to others and to Daphne, the use of the telephone by some of the monasteries and sketes, and the introduction of a few machines into certain of the monastic establishments, life on the Mountain today is what it was five centuries ago and even earlier. The monks live quietly, unhurriedly, peacefully, in the midst of unusually beautiful and healthy natural surroundings and in buildings that have been designed, not for the sake of bodily ease or vain display, but for the perfecting of the soul and the glorification of God. Life here has a simplicity, order, sincerity, meaningfulness and depth that it very seldom has in modern secularized society. Free from the confusion, distractions, anxiety and greed of contemporary civilization, the monks devote themselves to their simple tasks if they live in monasteries, to agriculture or handicrafts if they live in other monastic establishments, and above all to prayer. For those in «the world,» their mode of life is a great lesson in simple, harmonic living, in dedication to spiritual values, in constant striving for self-perfection and union with God.

During the last several decades, the number of Athonite monks has decreased markedly. Among the main causes of this have been the spread of materialistic doctrines in Greece and other countries, leading to a weakening and often the destruction of religious belief and feeling; the increasing secularization of society, that is, the increasing preoccupation with material values and the turning away from the spiritual; the promulgation of activistic doctrines, even within religious bodies, depreciating the contemplative life; and a series of wars involving Greece, which have repeatedly upset the Greek economic structure and seriously affected the finances of the monasteries. How to stop this unfortunate trend towards a decrease of the monastic population of Athos, and to increase the number of monks there, is the biggest and most vital problem that now concerns many Athonite monks. There are today about two thousand monks living in the twenty Athonite monasteries and their dependencies, whereas at the beginning of the century there were nearly seven and a half thousand. The problem, as the monks themselves see it, is not merely to increase their number, but especially to increase the number of *younger* monks. Senile monks have to be cared for and hence constitute a liability rather than an asset. The percentage of such monks is already too high. Younger monks, on the other hand, can perform various necessary tasks, learn more and benefit more.

Although serious, the problem is not one without parallel in the past, and it does not cause the monks to think that the Mountain will soon cease to be a living reality and become a mere library or museum. They recall, for instance, that after the Greek War of Independence more than a century ago, the number of monks on the Mountain was smaller than it is today. And they believe that this unique Pan-Orthodox democracy of monks will continue to exist until the end of time.

As to the measures that should be taken in order to reverse the present trend, they specify the following. First, steps should be taken to strengthen the piety of men. With increased piety in society, monasticism will be better appreciated and more men will feel disposed to embrace the monastic life. Secondly, the economic problem must be solved. The Greek government must furnish regularly adequate financial compensation to the monasteries for the estates it has expropriated. Thus, the monasteries will be able to provide satisfactorily for the needs of more members. Thirdly, bishops in Greece must stop taking monks from Athos and employing them as deacons, priests, and preachers of their dioceses. Instead, they should recruit novices for Athos. Finally, Athonite monks, as well as friends of Athos, should strive to provide a better understanding and appreciation of the ideals of Athonite monasticism.

Some important work has already been done by the monks of Athos to increase understanding. I referred earlier to the periodical *St. Paul of Xeropotamou* that is published by the Monastery of St. Paul, and to Theocletos' book on St. Nicodemos. This work, bearing the title *Saint Nicodemos the Aghiorite (Aghios Nicodemos o Aghioritis)* has already appeared in print. I should also mention another book by this monk, entitled *Between Heaven and Earth (Metaxi Ouranou kai Ghis)*, which appeared in 1956, and one by Archimandrite Gabriel, abbot of the Monastery of Dionysiou, entitled *The Voice of One Crying in the Wilderness (Phoni Voöntos ek tis Erimou)*, which was published in 1955. Theocletos' book *Between Heaven and Earth*, which is written in lively dialogue form, is an excellent interpretation and defence of Athonite monasticism. The author shows exceptional dialectical skill and literary talent, broad knowledge of the Church Fathers, and great religious fervor. Gabriel's book deals with a variety of subjects — ethical, social, and religious — and concludes with a very timely chapter on the Holy Mountain. I shall quote some of Gabriel's statements from this chapter. To the question that some have been asking, «What remains on the Holy Mountain?» he replies: «First of all, there remains the Holy Mountain, with its holy establishments, such as it was at the beginning, that is, with its monasteries, its sketes, its *kellia*, its hermitages fully functioning, with their same unaltered regulations *(typika)*, with its unshaken traditions and the religious love of God and neighbor. Second, in all these establishments the fathers strive to prove themselves, if not superior, at least worthy of their predecessors in the preservation and maintenance of the buildings....» Referring to the decrease in the number of monks, he says: «The splendor and grandeur of the Holy Mountain is not to be judged by the small or large number of monks who dwell on it. This fluctuation has occurred many times during its thousand year period of monastic life....» As to the economic problem, he remarks that «we positively hope that it will be settled....» Concerning the prospects of an increase in the number of monks, he says: «We Aghiorites steadfastly believe that our holy abodes on Mount Athos will soon be filled with monks.... We believe that the Mountain, by the Grace of God, will continue in existence till the end of time. The piety of Orthodox people will always envelop Athos, and souls beloved by God will never cease coming to it, because its spirituality will always have the power of attracting those who are heavy laden with sin, and its holiness, those who are pure in heart.»

GLOSSARY

Aghiorite. Of the Holy *(Aghion)* Mountain *(Oros)* or Mount Athos, Athonite.

Apódeipnon. The after-supper service, the compline.

Apolytíkion. A hymn used towards the end of the vesper service.

Apse. A projecting part of a church, internally semicircular. Although the main churches of the monasteries on Athos have three apses at the east end and also an apse on the north and on the south side, the term is generally employed to refer to the main eastern apse.

Arsanás (pl. *arsanádes*). A landing place (harbor or pier) with warehouses and other buildings.

Beautiful Gate. The door at the middle of the iconostasis, also known as the Holy Gate.

Dikaíos. The prior of a skete.

Dormition. Falling asleep; figuratively, death. St. Macarios the Great (300-390) says the following about the use of this term: «If one has passed from death to life, according to the esoteric teaching, he truly lives forever and does not die. Even if the bodies of such individuals are temporarily destroyed, they rise again in glory, for they have become sanctified. We therefore call the death of Christians dormition *(koimisis)*.»

Drum. The circular or polygonal wall that carries a dome.

Epítropos (pl. epítropoi). One of the committee of two or three senior monks who govern an idiorrhythmic monastery, or assist the abbot in governing a coenobitic monastery.

Esonarthex. The inner narthex of a church that has two narthexes.

Exonarthex. The outer narthex of a church.

Fresco. A painting executed on freshly spread moist plaster with pigments that have been mixed with water.

Gérontas. Elder.

Iconostasis. A wooden or marble screen, or a wall, supporting panel icons and separating the sanctuary *(bema)* from the main body of the church.

Kalyva (pl. kalyves). An isolated cottage or hut.

Katholikón. (pl. katholiká). The main church of a monastery.

Kellí (pl. kelliá). A monastic establishment consisting of a building with a chapel in it and some surrounding land, and usually inhabited by three monks; also, the cell of a monk.

Kontákion. A short *(kontós)* hymn chanted during the *orthros,* summarizing the significance of the holy day or the praise of the saint that is celebrated.

Kyriakón. The common church of a skete, where services are held for all the monks of the skete every Sunday *(Kyriaki)* and on the major holy days.

Liti. The inner narthex.

Liturgy. A service that corresponds to the Mass of the Latin Church.

Loukoum. A jellied sweet containing nuts and covered with powdered sugar.

Megalynárion. Usually, a verse taken from the Psalms of David and chanted during the matins, extolling and glorifying God; also a hymn composed by a Church hymnographer and chanted on a major holy day.

Mosaic. An icon or design made by inlaying small pieces of variously colored stone or glass.

Narthex. The west part of a church, in front of the nave, extending from the north to the south side of the building.

Nave. The main body of a church.

Oka. A weight, about 2³/₄ pounds.

Orthros. Matins.

Ouzo. A colorless liquor with anise flavor.

Panaghia. «The All-holy,» the Holy Virgin Mary.

Pantocrator. «The Ruler of All,» the Almighty.

Pendentive. The curved triangular area between adjoining arches that support a dome.

Perspective. The representation, on a plane or curved surface, of distant objects as they appear to the eye.

Phiale. The sacred fountain of a monastery, standing near the main church and consisting of a basin with a dome above it that rests on columns.

Proskynitárion. A stand on which special icons are set for veneration. Also a kiosk housing an icon.

Sémantron. A wooden or iron gong used at monasteries for announcing church services. It is suspended in the middle from a cord, or is carried, and is struck with a small wooden or iron hammer.

Skete. Typically, a settlement of hermits in the neighborhood of a common church, known as the *kyriakon,* by which is the dwelling of the *dikaios* or prior of the settlement and a guesthouse.

Theotókos. «She who gave birth to God,» the Holy Virgin Mary.

Tropárion. A hymn consisting of a single, rhythmic prose sentence. In most cases it is part of an ode and is patterned after the ode's first stanza, the hirmos.

Typikáris. The monk whose special task in church is to see to it that the services are conducted in strict conformity with the monastery's system of liturgical rules *(typikón).*

INDEX